52 Weeks
·of·
Worthiness

A year of practical advice
and biblical truth for claiming
your inherent value

Kristin Martinez

Copyright © 2017 Kristin Martinez

All rights reserved. No part of this book may be reproduced in any form or by an electronic or mechanical means, including information, storage and retrieval systems, without permission in writing from the publisher, except by reviewers, who may quote brief passages in a review.

ISBN 978-0-9993401-0-3 (Paperback Edition)
ISBN 978-0-9993401-1-0 (E-Book Edition)

Library of Congress Control Number: 2017913318

This work reflects the author's present recollections of experiences over time. Occasionally, names and persons in this book are entirely fictional and bear no resemblance to anyone living or dead. To protect the privacy of certain individuals some names and characteristics
have been changed.

Scripture quotations taken from the Amplified® Bible (AMP), Copyright © 2015 by The Lockman Foundation
Used by permission. www.Lockman.org

Scripture quotations taken from the Amplified® Bible (AMPC), Copyright © 1954, 1958, 1962, 1964, 1965, 1987 by The Lockman Foundation
Used by permission. www.Lockman.org

Scripture quotations are from the ESV® Bible (The Holy Bible, English Standard Version®), copyright © 2001 by Crossway, a publishing ministry of Good News Publishers. Used by permission. All rights reserved.

THE HOLY BIBLE, NEW INTERNATIONAL VERSION®, NIV® Copyright © 1973, 1978, 1984, 2011 by Biblica, Inc.® Used by permission. All rights reserved worldwide.

Scripture taken from *The Message*. Copyright © 1993, 1994, 1995, 1996, 2000, 2001, 2002. Used by permission of NavPress Publishing Group.

Scripture taken from the New King James Version®. Copyright © 1982 by Thomas Nelson. Used by permission. All rights reserved.

Scripture quotations are taken from The Living Bible copyright © 1971. Used by permission of Tyndale House Publishers, Inc., Carol Stream, Illinois 60188. All rights reserved.

Scripture quotations are from the Revised Standard Version of the Bible, copyright © 1946, 1952, and 1971 the Division of Christian Education of the National Council of the Churches of Christ in the United States of America. Used by permission. All rights reserved.

Editing by Susan Hulburt, Julie Osterman

Front cover design by Kim Hester
of Passionvine Creative

Book layout and design by Kim Hester
of Passionvine Creative

Printed and bound in USA
First Printing October 2017

Published by Ingram Spark
One Ingram Blvd.
La Vergne, TN 37086

DEDICATION

This book is dedicated to my husband, Rudy Martinez, without whose loving support it would not have been possible.

I feel blessed to have married a man who lives with Jesus Christ as his example, walking in love, humility, service and acceptance for others. I am especially grateful to you for honoring my faith in God, never doubting what I believe and feel called to act on for Him.

Your loving assurance for the work I do and constant encouragement have provided steadfastness when I needed it most.

Thank you for your gift of love and for bestowing the highest level of respect for me as your wife. I love you dearly.

CONTENTS

Introduction		11
WEEK 1	Identifying Your Core Values	15
WEEK 2	Honesty	21
WEEK 3	Remove Negative Labels	27
WEEK 4	Be Grateful	33
WEEK 5	Practice Humility (True Confessions)	39
WEEK 6	Move Past Your Mistakes	45
WEEK 7	Hold on to Hope	51
WEEK 8	Spend Time Alone	57
WEEK 9	Withdraw From the Competition	63
WEEK 10	Create a Positive File	69
WEEK 11	Keep Your Emotions in Balance	75
WEEK 12	Rest and Relaxation	81
WEEK 13	Lend an Ear (Listen)	87
WEEK 14	Maintain a Circle of Support	93
WEEK 15	Saying 'Yes' When You Should Say 'No'	99
WEEK 16	Extend Forgiveness	105

WEEK 17	Raining on the Inside	111
WEEK 18	Be Flexible in Your Mind	117
WEEK 19	Be True to Yourself	123
WEEK 20	Take an "I'm Sorry" Inventory	127
WEEK 21	Treat Yourself!	133
WEEK 22	Do Something Fun!	139
WEEK 23	Beauty Enhancements	145
WEEK 24	Put Things in Perspective	151
WEEK 25	Practice Acceptance	157
WEEK 26	Don't Let Anyone Steal Your Joy	163
WEEK 27	Love One Another	169
WEEK 28	Silence Your Worst Critic	175
WEEK 29	Never Stop Learning	181
WEEK 30	Proclaim Your Style	187
WEEK 31	Take Off the Mask	193
WEEK 32	Don't Be a Know It All	199
WEEK 33	Step Out of Your Comfort Zone	205
WEEK 34	Practice Decorum	211
WEEK 35	Perfection Is Not a Goal	217
WEEK 36	United We Stand	223
WEEK 37	Body Obsession	229
WEEK 38	Face Your Fears	235
WEEK 39	Respect	241
WEEK 40	Celebrating Alone But Not Lonely	245
WEEK 41	Health and Fitness	251
WEEK 42	Embrace Your Uniqueness	255

WEEK 43	Live Generously	261
WEEK 44	Clear the Clutter	265
WEEK 45	God's Opinion of You is What Matters Most	271
WEEK 46	Make the Most of It	277
WEEK 47	Stay Focused	281
WEEK 48	The Big E	287
WEEK 49	Celebrate Your Success	293
WEEK 50	It's Not Always About Being Right	299
WEEK 51	Know Your Limitations	305
WEEK 52	Leave a Legacy	311
Acknowledgments		317

INTRODUCTION

If SOMEONE WERE TO ASK YOU TO DEFINE SELF-WORTH, how would you respond? Chances are that you would answer based on how you are feeling today.

On any given day, we can experience a wide array of emotions. We may wake up feeling "on top of the world" with a great attitude, but by the end of the day our mindset has shifted downward and we have a negative perception of ourselves.

Many times we define our self-worth by our current situation. Our jobs, our status, who we hang out with, or even how others describe us often influence how we label ourselves.

Although these things can be a part of who we are, they don't define who we are. They don't define our self-worth. These are external influences, which we allow to determine whether or not we can feel good about ourselves.

External influences, or "worldly things," are temporary. They can affect our self-esteem.

Self-esteem can change based on external events.

Self-worth, though, is internal. It's a deeply rooted sense of knowing the true source of your usefulness and

value.

The fact that God created us places value on our lives. We were all created with a purpose. We each have our own gifts and unique talents. We are worth something. And we are worth something great!

Yet we continue the cycle of seeing how we measure up to someone else based on what we think is the model of a perfect _____. You fill in the blank.

In our society, there is a huge emphasis on outward appearances.

Most women (8 out of 10) and a growing number of men have a distorted view of themselves when they look into a mirror. We tend to use it as a flaw detector. Think about that for a moment. What did you say or think to yourself just this morning as you were getting dressed for the day?

If we know that we have value and that worthiness is something deeply rooted inside of us, why do we continue the struggle of feeling worthy on a daily basis? Let's face it, our world today is tough. We are confronted with many challenges and struggles. The expectations we place upon ourselves and others to be perfect, or at least near perfect, are extremely high and for the most part unattainable.

The following 52 chapters are designed to help you claim your worthiness each week throughout the year.

Included in each chapter is a weekly reflection, practical advice or exercises, and a challenge for the week.

Once you have completed Week 1, they may be used in any order or followed from start to finish. Jump from one to another if you choose. The intent of this book is to make it work for you! At the end of each chapter, a weekly focus of scriptures is listed. There are only a few each week. These scriptures have been prayerfully chosen and are designed to be taken in slowly. Read them, write them down, study them and let them speak to you. Come back to them and note how they may have applied to you during the week. I pray that you feel God's love for you poured out from these scriptures and know that you are worthy!

WEEK 1

IDENTIFYING YOUR CORE VALUES

ALTHOUGH THIS BOOK IS DESIGNED for you to begin from any week, I highly recommend reading this one first due to the importance of the exercise. When we can identify and honor our values, we can live a more balanced, authentic and peaceful life, and in turn, be true to our unique identity. Life presents us with choices to be made. An important part of the decision process stems from our values. Our core values, or principal beliefs, embody the things that matter most to us. This can be especially true when we are faced with difficult decisions or experiencing troublesome situations.

Do you know what your core values are? Type the phrase "personal core values" into your computer search engine and you will find a plethora of websites that lead you through charts and exercises to help you define your core values. I bet if you think about it, you can come up with a list of your own fairly quickly. Take a few moments to reflect:

- What are some things that have been important

to you for most of your life?

- Are these things just as important to you today?
- Can you recall a time when everything seemed to be in harmony? What was happening? How did you feel? What were you honoring at the time?

Now, let's take a deeper look and try to narrow the list down to 5-7 top core values:

- Besides your basic survival needs, what are some of the things that you need to feel your best?
- Are there some things that you would stand up for no matter what anyone else may say or do to change your mind?

Next, list them in order of their importance. You may need to take more time with this, perhaps even close the book and come back to it after a good night's rest.

Hopefully now you have an idea of your core values. Write them down and think about them, pray over them. You can use this list to help you in your decision process. Use it as a guide for when you should say "yes" and when you should say "no." Remind yourself not to compromise your core values. Honor them and practice them.

Far too many years for me were spent compromising my own core values. I knew deep down what was important to me, what mattered most and what made me feel my absolute best. Yet I continued saying "yes" to things that I knew that I should say "no" to, doing things I really did not want to do in order to avoid what I thought would result in a confrontation. I was agreeing to do things because I thought the person asking would like me more. Does any of this sound familiar? Once I learned to honor my core values, I discovered more peace and confidence in my life.

Honoring our core values is a continual process. Just as many successful companies operate by their mission statement, vision and values, we must do the same in our own lives and in our interactions with others. It is essential to take an inventory from time to time. Analyze if your day-to-day living is in sync with your core values:

- How do your daily activities reflect or conflict with your core values?

- Are your top core values representing both the person you are on the inside as well as how others may perceive you?

- Are there any areas where you feel the need to grow as an individual? What about along your spiritual path?

Challenge of the Week

Meet with a friend or acquaintance and plan "the perfect

day." It should include an entire day together, breakfast through dinner. Have fun with it, planning with no worries in mind! Make it something fun that you would love to do. Working together, keep in mind the following:

- Plan your day with three key things that matter to each one of you individually.

- Plan your day with three key things that you may also have in common with each other.

> *This is a fun exercise, and even more of a challenge when you don't know the other person as well as you might know a good friend. The idea here is to see just how much you practice honoring your values and needs during the process.

Focus for the Week

Proverbs 19:1 English Standard Version (ESV)

¹ Better is a poor person who walks in his integrity than one who is crooked in speech and is a fool.

Galatians 5:22-23 Living Bible (TLB)

²² But when the Holy Spirit controls our lives he will produce this kind of fruit in us: love, joy, peace, patience, kindness, goodness, faithfulness, ²³ gentleness and self-control; and here

there is no conflict with Jewish laws.

MATTHEW 16:26 ENGLISH STANDARD VERSION (ESV)

[26] For what will it profit a man if he gains the whole world and forfeits his soul? Or what shall a man give in return for his soul?

NOTES

WEEK 2

HONESTY

CHANCES ARE YOU'VE HEARD THE PHRASE "Honesty is the best policy." Maybe you have heard someone say that it "pays to be honest." These statements are in fact true, but not always easy to adhere to all of the time. Have you ever been invited somewhere or asked to do something and you already knew that you just couldn't do it or didn't want to? You may have had to think for a moment before you answered because you certainly didn't want to look bad or make the other person feel badly about the real reason you chose to decline. So you came up with an excuse, one that's not too far off from the real truth but not the whole truth either. Suppose you say that you cannot do something because of your schedule at the time. The opportunity may present itself again at another time that is convenient. Then you make another excuse. It happens again, and before long you are caught up in even more lies.

The point to make from this scenario is that in the long run you would feel better about yourself by telling the truth in the first place. It can be difficult. After all, we don't want to hurt someone else's feelings deliberately. Wouldn't it be better though to honor yourself and your boundaries or limitations? The other person would also know where you stand on a particular issue or preference. Say for example that you are invited to go to the movies and you cannot bear the thought of sitting through a movie in the theater, nor do you ever want to in the future. It would be best for someone to know that about you up front. This way, this particular friend will know not to ask you to go again.

Besides the desire to spare another person's feelings, why do we hold back from sharing the entire truth? I once viewed a presentation that described different types of lying and the behaviors that support them. For the most part, most of us lie to cover up something. We want to hide our flaws, bad habits or bad behavior. Among the top reasons were to gain an advantage somehow or for the benefit of ourselves or others. Low on the list was the malicious liar, one who deliberately is out to hurt someone or has cruel intentions.

Most of us mastered the craft of cover-up early on as children. Even though it is likely that we heard "do not lie" time and time again, we did it anyway. But in most of the situations in which we did lie, the truth eventually became exposed.

When we hold back from sharing the truth on a regular basis, we can quickly start perceiving it as something that is not so bad. We may tell ourselves that it was just a little white lie. But telling these little white lies can eventually become a habit, and before we realize it those little white lies grow into something bigger. When we fall into this pattern, our integrity is compromised. We feel our self-esteem lowering as a result. And worse, people may begin to see our weakened integrity on the outside as well.

There are also awkward situations that involve sharing the whole truth with other people to help them in some way. Perhaps you have an uncomfortable encounter with someone you happen to supervise at work or someone you are mentoring. In these instances it is vital to be gracious and tactful. Approach the situation from all perspectives. State your purpose of the discussion and what you hope to accomplish for all persons involved.

Honesty is something that is very important to me. In fact, it is among the top five on my list of core values. I often expect the same level of honesty from others, but it doesn't always happen that way. Let me also add that although I strive to be honest in all areas of my life, it's not always the easiest choice for me. I struggle with this issue just as everyone else does.

Challenge of the Week

Be mindful this week of your answers to others. Are you sincere in your response? Practice honesty in every aspect of your day-to-day activities. If you are facing a situation that could truly cause deep hurt to someone else, think and pray about it first. There are tactful, loving ways to share something that needs to be addressed.

Focus for the Week

Proverbs 11:1-2 New International Version (NIV)

¹The Lord detests dishonest scales,
but accurate weights find favor with him.

² When pride comes, then comes disgrace,
but with humility comes wisdom.

2 Timothy 2:15 Revised Standard Version (RSV)

¹⁵ Do your best to present yourself to God as one approved, a workman who has no need to be ashamed, rightly handling the word of truth

Ephesians 4:25 New International Version (NIV)

²⁵ Therefore each of you must put off falsehood and speak truthfully to your neighbor, for we are all members of one body.

NOTES

WEEK 3

REMOVE NEGATIVE LABELS

A LONGTIME FRIEND OF MINE AND HER COUSIN were both raised in homes where teasing and name calling among family members became part of the routine. My friend explained how many labels had been placed upon her over the years, some more hurtful than others. Although she knows that her family loves her, some of those names are just as fresh in her mind today as they were many years ago. Thankfully, neither one of these women has allowed the negative labels to define who they are inside.

Sadly, I know many other women who have allowed negative labels of the past to define their self-worth. I have heard countless stories from women who declare their future as negative in some way. Often while sharing their story, women will disclose their list of inadequacies based on labels that were placed upon them in the past. I've heard some women profess that they will never be able to get a certain job because they are just not smart enough. Other women are constantly recounting all of the instances in which they were called a name that was

Week 3: Remove Negative Labels

based upon their appearance to others.

During a discussion over coffee one day, a woman told me that she has vowed never to be fat again. As a child, this woman struggled with her weight and was always teased about it. Her mother did not offer much respite or comfort from the constant name-calling. Her mother stated that the teasing would stop if she would just lose some weight. I could see the pain in this woman's eyes as she shared her story with me. Through more of our discussion I learned that although she is grown up now and no longer struggles with her weight by any outside appearances, on the inside she is still that little girl being teased. This woman still wears the negative labels that she wore as a child. She desperately wanted to remove those labels, but she didn't know where to begin the process of removing them.

Many of us wear negative labels that have been placed upon us by others; however, we can remove them ourselves at any time. So how do we do this, especially after wearing them for so long? We can begin the process of healing by applying a shift in our mindset from negative thoughts to more positive ones:

- Stop using negative words about yourself. For instance, if you want to lose weight do it for the health benefits you will reap as a result, rather than saying, "I'm fat and need to lose weight."

- Declare and believe that you can do something if

you put your mind to it.

- Question the origin of your thoughts: Was this something that I thought about myself? Does it stem from a negative belief about myself based on what someone else has said about me in the past?

Challenge of the Week

Conduct a label exchange. Take an inventory this week of your various labels. Consider all of the times that you hear yourself referring to your negative label stock. Then place those names in your delete file. Next, determine how many positive labels you have. You may be surprised to find more than you thought you had. Save those positive labels in your file and hold on to them!

Focus for the Week

ISAIAH 43:18-19 THE MESSAGE (MSG)

¹⁸ "Forget about what's happened;
don't keep going over old history.
¹⁹ Be alert, be present. I'm about to do something brand-new.
It's bursting out! Don't you see it?
There it is! I'm making a road through the desert,

rivers in the badlands.

2 Corinthians 5:17-18 King James Version (KJV)

¹⁷ Therefore if any man be in Christ, he is a new creature: old things are passed away; behold, all things are become new.

¹⁸ And all things are of God, who hath reconciled us to himself by Jesus Christ, and hath given to us the ministry of reconciliation.

NOTES

WEEK 4

BE GRATEFUL

Thanksgiving is an important part of prayer. When we don't know what to say, we can always begin our prayer with gratitude. Have you ever noticed that once you start counting your blessings, you discover just how many there are in your life? Even in times of trial and sadness we can always find some reason to be grateful. There are situations that can make us feel like we have nothing to be grateful for in our lives. It's during these difficult times that we need gratitude the most.

Maintaining our appreciation throughout the day can become something that we don't think about too often. We may take for granted some of the routine things we are able to do. Reflect on all of our modern conveniences in our country that we don't give much thought. Running water, a warm bed and food on the table are what most would refer to as necessities, but this is not the case for many people in other parts of the world. Their needs also include water, food and shelter, but may vary by a significant degree. For instance, instead of running water from a faucet, they may have to depend on a limited supply of water that is brought in from somewhere else or have to walk several miles to get it themselves. Their sleeping quarters may consist of a small space on top of a heap of trash. Their food may not be on the table but found by scouring the streets for someone else's leftover scraps.

The uneven ratio of richness to poverty is something hard to understand. Many are living under poor conditions through no fault of their own. It is a sad truth to know that others are not able to have some of the luxuries that we may have. We can offer help by praying, even if we never meet some of these people. Another way to help is by providing support to organizations that have resources available to help in these areas. I could write an entirely different book on the heart-wrenching stories of poverty and people who have no place to call home.

Life seems unfair in so many ways. Although we cannot wave a wand and suddenly see the scales of this world magically balanced, we can practice gratitude. Being in a thankful state of mind helps to keep our minds fixed on more positive thoughts. Gratitude helps us realize what we have and may minimize our desire to acquire more material things. Do you know someone who always seems to be happy? People who exude happiness are grateful by nature.

Thankful thinking is one way to practice gratitude. We can also practice gratitude by verbally expressing thanks to others. We can say thank you to the service providers with whom we interact daily, weekly or monthly. We can say thank you to those who are closest to us. And we can say thank you to a total stranger. Where I live in Texas, it used to be common to wave a friendly tip of the hand as a gesture of thanks while driving on the road when someone allowed you to merge in front of them. That gesture is now a rare occurrence. I still use a little wave of thanks to fellow drivers on the road. Most of the time I do this, people don't seem to notice or even know what it means. I conclude that a lot of the time people immediately have their guard up, and assume that I am about to start an offensive exchange with the person in the other car. I do remember one occasion when another driver nodded back at me with a smile.

Practicing and expressing gratitude can be contagious. When we begin expressing our gratitude to others, they may start to reflect on some of the good things happening in their own life. Practice gratitude as much as you can; there is always a reason for us to give thanks. Say thank you often. The act of expressing sincere appreciation to someone may be just what they needed to feel better on a particular day.

Challenge of the Week

Try to refrain from complaining about things or criticizing as much as you can this week. If you slip a little, use it as an opportunity to find a way to reframe your focus into something that embodies gratitude.

Focus for the Week

Psalm 118:24 King James Version (KJV)

[24] This is the day which the Lord hath made; we will rejoice and be glad in it.

Colossians 2:7 English Standard Version (ESV)

[7] rooted and built up in him and established in the faith, just as you were taught, abounding in thanksgiving.

Psalm 136:26 Living Bible (TLB)

[26] Oh, give thanks to the God of heaven, for his loving-kindness continues forever.

NOTES

WEEK 5

PRACTICE HUMILITY
(TRUE CONFESSIONS)

Recently, I was in a store picking up a few groceries. As I approached the line, there was a man in front of me who was taking a lot of time as he checked out. He had many items and appeared to be annoyed or angry at someone. Then the man inquired about purchasing another item, causing the clerk to step away for a moment to retrieve what he wanted. I could not locate a divider to place down on the conveyor belt of the checkout, so I waited until there was enough space between our items before I started to unload mine. I could already feel the frustration building up inside me. *Kristin, be patient, you don't know anything about this man or what he is going through,* I told myself. As I was waiting, a lady came behind me with her cart, obviously anxious to get through the line quickly. *Oh great, now I am sandwiched between these two,* I thought. Moments later, the man in front of me completed his transaction and he was on his way. "Thank you; have a nice day," the clerk told him... But no response from the man, just grumbling as he left. The clerk at the register had such a sad expression after this.

As I approached the clerk, in what I felt was my best and hopefully encouraging demeanor, she began scanning my items. The lady behind me happened to find the divider and placed it on the conveyor belt. I looked up, somewhat perplexed but also humored. As we exchanged smiles, I said to her, "You have good eyes; I did not see that." That made me feel a bit better for the negative thoughts that had been occupying my head beforehand. As my transaction was just about complete, I noticed that one of the items that had been scanned did not belong to me. I quickly told the clerk but also felt that it was right to hand the item to the lady behind me. So I did. It was not a big deal to me; it was only a few dollars. But her reaction was priceless: She was so grateful and surprised! All of this, though, was the Holy Spirit working on me. What I needed that day was not more time, or an expedited process. What I truly needed was a reminder to always show kindness and understanding to others.

Think about the power of the Holy Spirit. In just a matter of a few minutes and in such an everyday setting, here were three people with whom I had interactions, each one with different burdens and life challenges. We never know when and where the Holy Spirit wants to use us to bless others or to lift them up in some small way.

Perhaps you have experienced something similar. When you think back on the experience, can you recall the faces of the people with whom you had interactions during the day? What burdens might they have been carrying?

Challenge of the Week

Look for opportunities to bless others. It doesn't have to, nor will it always, be in a big way. The world needs you to be light in many ways, helping to make it a better place. Be in tune with your daily interactions with others. Chances are you will find new opportunities!

Focus for the Week

> PHILIPPIANS 2:3-7 ENGLISH STANDARD VERSION (ESV)
>
> ³ Do nothing from rivalry or conceit, but in humility count others more significant than yourselves. ⁴ Let each of you look not only to his own interests, but also to the interests of others. ⁵ Have this mind among yourselves, which is yours in Christ Jesus, ⁶ who, though he was in the form of God, did not count equality with God a thing to be grasped, ⁷ but made himself nothing, taking the form of a servant, being born in the likeness of men.
>
> COLOSSIANS 3:12 KING JAMES VERSION (KJV)

¹² Put on therefore, as the elect of God, holy and beloved, bowels of mercies, kindness, humbleness of mind, meekness, longsuffering.

PHILIPPIANS 2 REVISED STANDARD VERSION (RSV)

¹ So if there is any encouragement in Christ, any incentive of love, any participation in the Spirit, any affection and sympathy, ² complete my joy by being of the same mind, having the same love, being in full accord and of one mind. ³ Do nothing from selfishness or conceit, but in humility count others better than yourselves. ⁴ Let each of you look not only to his own interests, but also to the interests of others. ⁵ Have this mind among yourselves, which is yours in Christ Jesus, ⁶ who, though he was in the form of God, did not count equality with God a thing to be grasped, ⁷ but emptied himself, taking the form of a servant, being born in the likeness of men. ⁸ And being found in human form he humbled himself and became obedient unto death, even death on a cross. ⁹ Therefore God has highly exalted him and bestowed on him the name which is above every name, ¹⁰ that at the name of Jesus every knee should bow, in heaven and on earth and under the

earth, [11] and every tongue confess that Jesus Christ is Lord, to the glory of God the Father.

GALATIANS 5:22-23 ENGLISH STANDARD VERSION (ESV)

[22] But the fruit of the Spirit is love, joy, peace, patience, kindness, goodness, faithfulness, [23] gentleness, self-control; against such things there is no law.

NOTES

WEEK 6

MOVE PAST YOUR MISTAKES

Get over it! We've all heard this at some point in our life. Do we know what it means? To get over something means to put it behind us, or forget. More often than not, we can't put something behind us. This is particularly the case when we are hanging on to past mistakes, those mistakes we made a long time ago that others most likely have forgotten. But *we* haven't forgotten. We can still remember all the details of the mistake so clearly in our minds.

God's word tells us to forgive and forget. We can forgive and forget the mistakes that others may make, yet have a difficult time forgiving ourselves for our mistakes. It can be hard for us to forget the hurt we may have caused. We can easily slide into the mind game of saying, "I should've, would've or could've done ___." The guilt we carry from our past mistakes can become such a heavy weight on our shoulders. This "guilt trip" is one that I have taken quite often myself, but I have learned how to pack for this trip so that I won't stay there very long.

Week 6: Move Past Your Mistakes

How often have you found yourself replaying a scenario in your head, wishing that you had done things differently? Most of the time, there are limited options available for us to change something that has happened in the past. We can always offer an apology if the situation warrants one. It's always best to acknowledge our mistakes, correct them in any way that we can and move on. Oh, but then the worrying in our mind comes along: *How bad I must have looked to everyone else when I made that horrible mistake.* Our thoughts may become so intently focused on how we appear to others that soon we have convinced ourselves that the mistake is much worse than in reality.

I have made many mistakes in my lifetime, just like everyone else. I will continue to make mistakes going forward in my life. In hindsight, I can see that many of the mistakes from my past have been opportunities for me to learn something. I have learned how to do some things better, what not to do in certain situations, and many other valuable lessons. And there are some mistakes I have made that just make me laugh at myself (in a good way) when I think about them.

Perhaps some of the regrettable things of your past have taught you lessons along the way as well. Rather than dwelling on the negative aspect of your mistakes, look at them from a learning perspective or as a turning point in your life. Begin the process by taking ownership of your mistakes. Don't try to rationalize them or turn the blame outwardly toward someone else.

Everyone makes mistakes. We are not perfect. Many accomplished people experienced a multitude of errors before they ultimately found success. When we set goals for ourselves, it's likely that we will encounter setbacks from a mistake or two along the way. The main thing to keep in perspective is that we are moving ahead, learning and growing from each mistake that we make.

Most importantly, I want you to remember that *you* are not the mistake. The mistake is something you did; it does not define who you are. Remembering this will help you move forward past the mistake.

Challenge of the Week

Is there something new that you have been wanting to explore but have not because you thought it might be beyond your capability? Try something new, even if you make a mistake or it doesn't go as well as you thought it would.

Focus for the Week

Psalm 37:23-24 English Standard Version (ESV)

> ²³ The steps of a man are established by the Lord,
> when he delights in his way;
> ²⁴ though he fall, he shall not be cast headlong,

for the LORD upholds his hand.

PROVERBS 24:16 REVISED STANDARD VERSION (RSV)

¹⁶ for a righteous man falls seven times, and rises again;
but the wicked are overthrown by calamity.

PHILIPPIANS 3:13 NEW KING JAMES VERSION (NKJV)

¹³ Brethren, I do not count myself to have apprehended; but one thing *I do,* forgetting those things which are behind and reaching forward to those things which are ahead.

NOTES

WEEK 7

HOLD ON TO HOPE

Have you ever hoped for something for what seemed to be an extended period, then finally lost your hope and gave up?

Many of us have experienced a time like this. Deep in despair, wondering if there was any light on the other side while in the midst of this trial. When you reflect back on times like these, what brought you through to find hope once again? Or perhaps you never did and only remember getting through this troublesome experience with the passing of time.

Either way, it is imperative for us to hold on to hope. Cling to it. Sometimes it's all we have. Sometimes we are the only ones who have it. But we must not let it go. Jesus tells us to have hope. Without hope, we have no power to overcome our feelings of despair.

But what about all of the times we have hoped for something and it never turned out the way that we hoped it would?

This is when we need to be sure of *Christian* hope, in place of *worldly* hope:

- When we hope for something in our world, we are anticipating that our desire may be fulfilled. But we don't know with all certainty that it will be fulfilled. We might say, "I hope _____ happens." Or, "I hope everything goes well."

We're full of hope and for the most part also filled with anticipation that there will be a good outcome.

- Christian hope, though, is rooted in expectation. The expectation is stronger than anticipation. It is not only desiring something good but also expecting it to happen. Christian hope is knowing God's promise and trusting the promise. It is having confidence that something will transpire because God said that it would.

You might be saying to yourself, *Well, I don't know what God's promises are* or *How can I have hope when I have had nothing but disappointment?* Begin by reading what God's word from the Bible says about hope. There are many scriptures written about hope. Or search on your computer for the words "biblical hope" or "Christian hope." You will find many scriptures on the subject. When you are in the midst of a trial, remind yourself that something good can come out of a bad situation. Your current situation does not necessarily dictate your future position. God is always at work, even when we don't see anything happening. He has our best interests at heart and intends not to harm us, but to give us hope and a future.

Spend some time to reflect:

- Recall the times when something good happened. Something that you had hoped for did come to pass.

- God did something amazing, perhaps even when you weren't anticipating anything at all.

- Hope can sometimes come to us through someone else. Have you ever received a sudden, unexpected note of encouragement or an uplifting call from a friend, just when you needed it the most?

A sincere smile from a stranger can do wonders to lift us up. We can also provide hope to others. A hug, a smile or just a listening heart can bring hope to someone who is so desperately seeking it.

God's word provides hope. Hope is what keeps us going. When we get out of bed each day, we can have hope. It's not always easy to grasp, but it is ours to have as a gift from God.

Hope is our strength. We may have had the worst day, feeling like there is no hope. We can hope for something great and still have an adverse outcome. Chronic illness, loss of a loved one or disappointment from the expectations that we have placed on others can leave us feeling as if we have hoped in vain, *hopelessly* hoping, with nothing good as a result. But when we rely on our Christian hope, knowing with full confidence that God has our backs on this one, we can experience true hope. From hope we can also experience peace. Hope and peace will provide us the strength to forge ahead no matter what, and the opportunity to extend grace to others, just as God does to us. The outcome may not be what we thought it would be, but we can fully rely on the promises of God, knowing that we are worthy of his love and grace. And he is our ally in every situation that we encounter.

Challenge of the Week

In many instances, we lose our hope when our minds are worn out and overburdened with negative thoughts. It can be hard to think of hopeful things. Take time to listen to God and His word. Ask God what His promises are for you. Write your Book of Hope. It can be as simple as starting with a small pocket-sized notepad. Jot down all of the hopeful things in your life. Look back at the reflections listed here, and create a list of all the good things you have experienced. Hope is yours; it's in your future even if you don't feel it now!

Focus for the Week

JEREMIAH 29:11-13 LIVING BIBLE (TLB)

[11] For I know the plans I have for you, says the Lord.

They are plans for good and not for evil, to give you a future and a hope. ¹² In those days when you pray, I will listen. ¹³ You will find me when you seek me, if you look for me in earnest.

Romans 5:1-5 English Standard Version (ESV)

¹ Therefore, since we have been justified by faith, we have peace with God through our Lord Jesus Christ. ² Through him we have also obtained access by faith into this grace in which we stand, and we rejoice in hope of the glory of God. ³ Not only that, but we rejoice in our sufferings, knowing that suffering produces endurance, ⁴ and endurance produces character, and character produces hope, ⁵ and hope does not put us to shame, because God's love has been poured into our hearts through the Holy Spirit who has been given to us.

1 Corinthians 13:6-7 Revised Standard Version (RSV)

⁶ it does not rejoice at wrong, but rejoices in the right. ⁷ Love bears all things, believes all things, hopes all things, and endures all things.

NOTES

WEEK 8

SPEND TIME ALONE

Some people think that spending time alone is a bad thing. Sure, there are instances in which being alone too much of the time can be harmful. We all need the community of others. Our relationships with other people are important for our nurturing and well-being. Some people thrive on being around others all of the time. There are others who like to be alone for one reason or another. Some people become lonely if no one else is around.

Wherever you fall in this category, there is no right or wrong, just a matter of preference. There are introverted people and extroverted people. The key is to have the right balance in regards to your emotional welfare. There are many benefits to gain from spending time alone:

- *Time alone provides an excellent opportunity to recharge your mind.* The demands of our day can zap our energy levels and leave our minds in a state of frenzy. Your mind may be racing with an inventory of thoughts from the meetings and phone conversations you have had to deal with during the day. Spending time alone for a few minutes at the end of a work day can help you transition more smoothly into the time you spend at home.

- *Time alone can help you connect with your creative side.* Many times our best ideas come from the time we spend alone with our thoughts. It is a good thing to brainstorm sometimes, but other peoples' voices can also become a distraction to your own thoughts.

- *Time alone may help you appreciate others more.* Your time apart from family and friends may help you see them in a better light, realizing all that they do for you and how much they mean to you. The time you spend with family and friends becomes more valuable to you.

- *Time alone is a fantastic way to discover some of your likes and dislikes.* When you are alone, there is no need to consult with others about the agenda. You can choose how to spend your time, doing something that you enjoy.

Do you consider yourself an introverted person or an extroverted person? Maybe you possess traits from both personality types. Personally, I fall in the middle of the two. I love being around people, but I also enjoy my time alone, away from everyone else. No matter which personality type you relate to more, it is important for you to embrace time alone for yourself. We all have so much going on around us and so many things that drain our energy. When we spend time alone and recharge our bodies and minds, we can be fully engaged in the time we have with others. Being engaged with others is a vital part of honoring the relationship we have with them.

Challenge of the Week

Spend at least one day this week completely disconnected from your computer, phone and television. Don't check any of your social media apps. Use your time away from technology just to relax, reflect on things or give more attention to a project or hobby that you have put aside.

Focus for the Week

> PSALM 46:10 NEW INTERNATIONAL VERSION (NIV)
>
> [10] He says, "Be still, and know that I am God;
> I will be exalted among the nations,
> I will be exalted in the earth."

Week 8: Spend Time Alone

LAMENTATIONS 3:27-28 REVISED STANDARD VERSION (RSV)

> ²⁷ It is good for a man that he bear
> the yoke in his youth.
>
> ²⁸ Let him sit alone in silence
> when he has laid it on him.

NOTES

WEEK 9

WITHDRAW FROM THE COMPETITION

Have you ever thought about how much time you spend in competition with others? Many times we may feel the need to blend in or gain acceptance based on how we look on the outside. Advertising campaigns and social media postings can quickly have us assessing our wardrobe to determine whether or not we're on target with the latest fashion trends. Personally, I must admit that I have had days where I spent far too much time staring into my closet full of clothes, wondering, "What shall I wear?" Even though I had much to choose from, I was concerned about how I would look to others. I was also trying to compete. Maybe you know the drill: *That certain someone is going to be there today, and I must find the perfect outfit to enter the room with full confidence.* Wow, did I really think that? It took a lesson for me to realize how much emphasis was being placed on my outward appearance:

Staring into my closet one day, I heard a message in my head: *You're spending too much time worrying about what*

Week 9: Withdraw from the Competition

you will wear. To which I thought, *OK, I know, but ....* I was trying to find that perfect outfit. It was one of those days when I had several commitments stretching into the late evening. *Hmmm, now what can I put on that is comfortable, practical and yet oh so stylish? Yay, finally found the one!* As I was just about ready and pushing it to the last minute, I might add, once again I heard that voice in my head: *You're too worried about how you look. Just get going.* I was finally ready and not a moment to spare. Keys in hand, beverage for the road, finally in the car and right on schedule! Early on along the drive, I took a sip of my drink. To my dismay, I discovered the lid on my beverage was not completely closed as it spilled all over my outfit, part of which was white, and also part of which was new. *Oh no, now what I am going to do?* I knew it would not come out quickly, so I had no choice but to turn around and head back home. I rushed to the door, quickly changed into something else and tossed the stained outfit into the sink with some water. Due to this mishap, I was late for my first appointment. When I came back home later that evening I checked on the outfit, which I thought would be ruined. It was OK, but what a lesson I learned that day!

Here I was worrying more about outward appearances instead of inward appearances. I already had what I needed to clothe myself with compassion, kindness, humility, gentleness and patience, as advised in Colossians 3:12.

Reflecting back, as I went through the events of the

day, nothing that I experienced had anything to do with what I was wearing on the outside and everything to do with what was on the inside. In preparation for the day, I was seeking affirmation from others through compliments or kind thoughts, perhaps. I had to ask myself if I was dressing a certain way to feel as if I were on the same level as someone else, or worse yet, above them.

It is not always our choice of clothing that will catapult us into the competition mode. We compete with our status, our homes, our cars, material possessions and job titles ... even our children and their accomplishments, dare I say.

When we scroll through the social media postings of our friends, we can easily feel less-than perfect in some way. They may be wearing the *perfect* outfit in front of the *perfect* home and be with the *perfect* family. Don't let that "highlight" of someone else's life deem what is realistic in everyday life. Most of us only post the good things in our lives, like vacations and exciting news to share. It's natural for us to want to look our absolute best to others in every way. Remember, though, that to *show* your absolute best you must first *feel* your best on the inside.

When we focus on the inside and feel good about ourselves, we allow a positive self-esteem to flow and naturally shine out to others, no matter what outfit we're wearing.

Do you ever feel that you are spending too much time focusing on your outward appearance?

- What will I wear?
- What will others think of my outfit?
- Is it fashionable?
- Does it make me look ___?

Challenge of the Week

Ask God to help you as you get dressed each day. Ask Him to help you find an outfit that is pleasing to him. He knows what is best for you. Take an inventory of your closet. Look for clothes that you may have purchased with someone else in mind or under another person's influence, against your better judgment. Then pass them along, donating or recycling. Also, consider clothes that you love no matter what someone else has said about them (although please practice modesty and decorum here). Be mindful of your inner beauty and all that you have to offer.

Focus for the Week

> Colossians 3:12 English Standard Version (ESV)
>
> [12] Put on then, as God's chosen ones, holy and beloved, compassionate hearts, kindness, humility, meekness, and patience ....

1 Samuel 16:7 Living Bible (TLB)

⁷ But the Lord said to Samuel, "Don't judge by a man's face or height, for this is not the one. I don't make decisions the way you do! Men judge by outward appearance, but I look at a man's thoughts and intentions."

2 Corinthians 5:12 New International Version (NIV)

¹² We are not trying to commend ourselves to you again, but are giving you an opportunity to take pride in us, so that you can answer those who take pride in what is seen rather than in what is in the heart.

NOTES

WEEK 10

CREATE A POSITIVE FILE

In our world today, we are surrounded by negativity, especially in the news. At times it can seem nearly impossible to read or hear about anything good.

We can be negative too. We are quick to complain and much of the time focused on the bad instead of the good. We tend to do this with ourselves too. If someone compliments us, we don't always accept it just as we should. And why is it that no matter how many positive things we may hear about ourselves, we focus much of our energy on the negative things that may have been said?

Several years ago, I had a sales position within a large corporation. The goals in place for my department seemed to be far reaching at times. Working in sales can be extremely competitive and stressful. In my department, we had a weekly sales report with everyone's results posted for all to see. I'll be honest, that was agonizing for me! One week I would be among the top, and the very next week I might be listed on the bottom of the chart. By the grace of God I did manage to do OK, meeting my goals. However, I was never able to exceed them and be recognized as a "top performer." Here I was doing the job that I was expected to do, yet I always felt somewhat inadequate. I had a great rapport with my clients and among my peers, but still felt that I did not quite measure up due to my sales performance.

One day as I was organizing my desk, I found some cards and kudos from coworkers and clients that I had saved over time, along with inspirational quotes and cards. Doing this gave me an idea to take all of them and create a file of pick-me-ups. So I made a new folder and labeled it "My Positive File." Anytime I felt down or inadequate, I would reach into that folder and quickly feel better. That was great, but I still felt that I needed some tangible way to remind me of the accomplishments I had made to reach my sales goals. So I found a beautiful flower vase from home, went to a local dollar store and bought a bag of crystal colored marbles. I placed the vase on top of my desk, and each time I closed a deal I added a marble to the jar. Soon it became full of marbles and it looked so beautiful, especially when rays from the sun through the window would shine on the marbles and look like rainbows. That was my little affirmation jar. It was also a great conversation piece. I still have it today!

My friend recently lost her spouse and she was in need of a reminder for all of the good things in her life. I bought her a clay jar and started it off with a note. Her task is to fill it by the end of the year. I have seen similar ideas for New Year's Eve parties too. You could begin the year with an empty jar or container and fill it with good things that you consider blessings throughout the year.

We can shift our focus from the negative to the positive. It takes some time but the effort is well worth it. Our positive attitude can do wonders to lift others up and lift our spirits as well.

Challenge of the Week

Your challenge this week is the same as the chapter title: Create a Positive File. It doesn't need to be anything elaborate. You can even look on craft websites or in stores for ideas. Have fun with your creation. Make it something that you will enjoy looking at and feel good in knowing what it represents to you.

Focus for the Week

Philippians 4:8 English Standard Version (ESV)

⁸ Finally, brothers, whatever is true, whatever is honorable, whatever is just, whatever is pure, whatever is lovely, whatever is commendable, if there is any excellence, if there is anything worthy of praise, think about these things.

Proverbs 18:20 Revised Standard Version (RSV)

[20] From the fruit of his mouth a man is satisfied; he is satisfied by the yield of his lips.

Romans 12:2 Revised Standard Version (RSV)

[2] Do not be conformed to this world but be transformed by the renewal of your mind, that you may prove what is the will of God, what is good and acceptable and perfect.

NOTES

WEEK 11

KEEP YOUR EMOTIONS IN BALANCE

Emotions are the feelings that we experience throughout the day. Our emotions are an instinctive state of mind and can fluctuate depending on our circumstances. On any given day we may experience an array of emotions: happiness, sadness, excitement and anger, to name just a few. Think about the emoticon libraries that are available to us through email accounts, social media and our cell phones. We don't even have to express our feelings through words. Just click on the little face sticker that applies best to your current state of mind and everyone instantly knows how you are feeling.

Some people may find it easier to share their emotions than others. You've heard the adage, "She wears her heart on her sleeve." Such a person would be more vulnerable to her emotions, allowing everyone to see the feelings that she is experiencing at the moment.

Each of us will experience things differently from one another. What makes you feel angry may not affect someone else in the same way. Your friend may become excited about something; you, however, do not share her excitement in any way. In some instances, the same issue we have experienced once can come up again later and we find ourselves feeling differently than we did before. Have you experienced a time like this? The emotions we experience can fluctuate depending on the circumstances around us. They can also be affected by our physical state. Perhaps you can recall a time when you felt as if you were carrying the weight of the world on your shoulders and believed that no one else had ever experienced what you were feeling at the time. Your challenge seemed insurmountable to overcome. There appeared to be no hope at all. Then, on another occasion, you viewed the same situation from a more positive stance. Or how about the time when you were in the middle of a regular discussion and suddenly found yourself saying hurtful things that you did not intend to say?

This last scenario can leave us feeling badly. Our mood level can quickly shift into a downward spiral. Our mind begins the process of questioning our right to claim our worthiness. During times like these, we need to be aware of our thoughts and feelings especially. We need to "check in" with our feelings.

The idea of checking in on your feelings may seem a little strange. It can feel uncomfortable to experience silence, especially when we are in the middle of a conversation. Our words, though, can have a lasting effect, both good and bad. It is important to allow yourself a moment or two to pause and reflect on something you are about to say to someone else. Take time also to reflect when you are alone and questioning why you may be feeling down, angry or even resentful.

In many instances our reaction to a situation is in direct connection with our physical state. The next time you are experiencing a major downswing in your mood, think about the reason why you may be feeling this way. Are you tired, maybe to the point of exhaustion? Is there a chance that you are tense about something else? Have you been able to get enough physical activity? Are you hungry or thirsty? Ask yourself these questions. Sometimes just stepping away for a breath of fresh air can do wonders for our minds. Even taking a break to get a drink of water can be beneficial to our emotional state.

As we cover the topic of Rest and Relaxation in Week 12, I list an example of the negative effects we can experience from lack of sleep. Most of the time when we are feeling negative it is due to our emotions being out of balance in some area.

But how do we keep our emotions in balance? One of the easiest things to remember is that most of the time we are *reacting* to something rather than *responding* to it. When someone asks a question that we do not know how to answer, the easy thing might be to say something, anything, just to give an answer. We may feel a knee-jerk reaction to provide an answer immediately. However, pausing for a moment will allow us to more appropriately respond to the question. It is fine to answer, "I don't know." This is a response instead of a reaction.

If we're facing a dangerous situation, our first instinct is to react to protect our well-being. I think it's safe to say that we would *all* be in reaction mode if we're facing a life-threatening situation. This survival mode is part of who we are as humans. And as human beings, we are emotional beings too. We cry, we laugh and we become frustrated, angry and depressed at times. The key thing to remember is that these are all feelings, and we can keep our emotions from taking control of our lives. In most instances, with practice we can influence our minds to take the positive road over a more negative one.

Emotions are healthy. They are a part of us. Our emotions allow us to fully experience life along with its high points, low points and all the places in-between. The bad times will come. We all have storms brewing out there somewhere. But we can still sail through them to the other side. We can keep our emotions in healthy balance by taking control of them in the best way we can.

Challenge of the Week

Journaling is an excellent way to capture your thoughts and feelings. This week, write in a journal. List your activities of the day. Recall the memorable moments of your day, good or bad. Make a note of how you are feeling. List any mood swings that you may have experienced. Are you happy, tired or feeling anxious? It is enlightening to come back later and read how you felt on that particular day. Look for patterns in your moods and take notes. Is there any outcome in which you feel you are in control? What are some of the things that you cannot control?

Focus for the Week

ROMANS 12:2 LIVING BIBLE (TLB)

² Don't copy the behavior and customs of this world, but be a new and different person with a fresh newness in all you do and think. Then you will learn from your own experience how his ways will really satisfy you.

PROVERBS 29:11 ENGLISH STANDARD VERSION (ESV)

¹¹ A fool gives full vent to his spirit,
but a wise man quietly holds it back.

NOTES

WEEK 12

REST AND RELAXATION

JUST THINKING ABOUT THE WORD "REST" can make us feel good, reflecting on all that the word encompasses. *Ah, but if only...* we might say to ourselves as if we need to give up something from our busy routines to allow time for us to have adequate rest. What amount of rest is sufficient? Most experts agree that sleeping for 6-8 hours per night on a regular basis defines proper rest. Sleep is vital to our health and well-being. It helps our bodies and minds to function at their best level. Rest does not only mean to sleep; we can rest by taking a break. We may think first about rest for our bodies, but rest for our minds is just as important.

Women are especially prone to have several thoughts racing in their heads at the same time. Our minds can go into overload mode. Besides this, we may also run our bodies to their maximum level, to the point of exhaustion and, from time to time, making ourselves sick. I have experienced this on some occasions. My body kept telling me to stop, slow down, but I kept pushing myself. Then I became ill and had no choice but to rest and gain my strength back.

When we are tired from lack of sleep or overload from our day-to-day busyness, we are prone to react to things with more anxiety and stress than we normally would had we been fully rested. Think about those times when your situation just seemed to have no resolution, and as your restless nights added up to a greater lack of sleep things appeared to be unbearable to handle. After one night of restful sleep, or even over the course of a few days, your perspective changed a little. Although the issue was still there, you somehow felt a bit more positive about it. What about those times when you started to cry over a seemingly trivial issue and said, "I don't know why I am crying over this." Chances are you reacted this way because you are overly tired.

Some instances justify a person's tears. Some of us are more prone than others to cry under a given circumstance. Personally, I can be watching a movie and during a touching scene feel the lump in my throat and tears in my eyes beginning to well up. I used to apologize for being this way, but now I just accept it. I have also experienced those times of crying over what seemed to be an awful situation, and after a good night's sleep I perceived it from a more positive viewpoint. This change of perspective allowed me the wisdom and insight to make the best decision or determine the best solution possible.

Many people feel that they just don't have the time to rest, almost bragging about how busy and important they are to everyone. They might refer to their jobs, their family and their ongoing commitments. So many are caught up in how they look to everyone else and they view rest as unproductive, perhaps even as loafing.

Adequate rest allows us to function properly and live a more balanced, productive life. Do you remember the age-old story of the tortoise and the hare? The tortoise won because he allowed himself adequate rest along the way, not wearing himself out. More important to remember is that God wants us to rest. In the book of Genesis, where the story of creation is written, it says that on the seventh day, God rested. Jesus also frequently took time out, away from everyone else, to rest and to spend some time in prayer and meditation.

Challenge of the Week

Find time this week to take a break. There's no need to plan any agenda for this time. Just sit quietly for a few moments. Rest and focus on positive thoughts in your mind. If you are in the middle of a difficult task or mounting deadline, stop and take a short break. Allow your mind and body to rest. As I am writing this book, I am also accepting this challenge to take a break!

Focus for the Week

MARK 6:31 LIVING BIBLE (TLB)

Week 12: Rest and Relaxation

³¹ Then Jesus suggested, "Let's get away from the crowds for a while and rest." For so many people were coming and going that they scarcely had time to eat.

Luke 5:15-16 English Standard Version (ESV)

¹⁵ But now even more the report about him went abroad, and great crowds gathered to hear him and to be healed of their infirmities. ¹⁶ But he would withdraw to desolate places and pray.

Genesis 2:2 New International Version (NIV)

² By the seventh day God had finished the work he had been doing; so on the seventh day he rested from all his work.

NOTES

WEEK 13

LEND AN EAR
(LISTEN)

SEVERAL YEARS AGO, I EXPERIENCED FIRSTHAND the power of someone else sitting across from me and intently listening as I shared my story. It was during a time of transformation for me; I was in a support group and each of us were partnered with another person who served as an accountability sponsor, someone who was there to help keep us accountable in our faith walk and to help with our day-to-day challenges and struggles. They were to come alongside us and support us in good times and bad. I was in the middle of a divorce at the time. My sponsor and I would meet each week at a local coffee shop to discuss any high points or low points and any obstacles that I needed help to overcome. Before one of our meetings, I was assigned an exercise to help with mapping out my story. It also included reflecting on times when I may have needed to ask for forgiveness, extend forgiveness or both. The sharing from my writing of it all took just about the whole hour of our meeting time. Not once did my sponsor try to interrupt me, or even of-

Week 13: Lend an Ear (Listen)

fer advice or words of comfort. She just quietly listened with a caring ear. It was an incredible experience, one that I will always remember and hopefully always strive to do the same for others. It seemed like such a rarity, especially in our busy, noisy world today. Everyone wants to speak, and everyone wants his or her voice to be heard by others.

Often we are thinking about what we are going to say while someone else is still speaking. Is that listening? A substantial amount of our conversations become distorted or exaggerated from the lack of fully listening. How about those times when a friend shared some news or a story with you and later you discovered that there was more to it than you initially heard? Or maybe there was an instance when you conveyed a specific request to someone with explicit details, only to discover that the result was not at all what you had asked.

I think it's safe to say that we have all been there. It can be discouraging, to say the least. While we can't control the thoughts and actions of others, we can control our own. Did you know that the words "listen" and "silent" both contain the same letters, just arranged in a different sequence? By remaining silent, we can hear others. When you actively listen to someone else, it is a gift to them. Numerous people are hurting and want someone just to hear them. They need someone to lend an ear, to listen to them without giving advice or telling them about a similar experience or situation.

Mastering the art of listening is not always easy. But there are ways to make a conscious effort while practicing this skill. Begin by understanding what the other person is saying to you. Ask for clarification if it is needed for you to comprehend what they mean. If the conversation involves some business assignments or important matters, don't hesitate to take notes. Let the other person know that you are taking notes to be clear about what they are saying. Validate what you heard. "I heard you say ___. Is that correct?" or "When you said ___, did you mean ___?"

Attentive listening is a valuable skill to possess. Remember that listening with intent, perhaps with the occasional nod during a conversation, does not mean that you necessarily agree with everything that the other person is saying. You are only listening until it is your turn to speak. The expertise of listening is not only a skill but also a dignified and respectful courtesy to others. Offer it freely, without any expectations; it's truly a gift to the person as you sincerely listen to his or her words.

Challenge of the Week

This week, take the time to listen. Be silent while someone else speaks, and reflect on the conversation afterward.

- Was there anything that you learned from the conversation?

Week 13: Lend an Ear (Listen)

- Did anything that was said surprise you in any way?

Listen also to yourself. Allow your inner voice to speak. Listen to your heart. Ask God what He wants you to hear. Take at least 15-20 minutes to sit in silence. It may feel awkward at first, but in time the art of listening will become easier for you to master.

Focus for the Week

James 1:19 Revised Standard Version (RSV)

¹⁹ Know this, my beloved brethren. Let every man be quick to hear, slow to speak, slow to anger.

1 Samuel 15:22-23 The Message (MSG)

²² Then Samuel said,
Do you think all God wants are sacrifices—
   empty rituals just for show?
He wants you to listen to him!
Plain listening is the thing,
   not staging a lavish religious production.
²³ Not doing what God tells you
   is far worse than fooling around in the occult.
Getting self-important around God

>   is far worse than making deals with your dead
>   ancestors.
> Because you said No to God's command,
>   he says No to your kingship.

1 JOHN 5:14 LIVING BIBLE (TLB)

> [14] And we are sure of this, that he will listen to us whenever we ask him for anything in line with his will.

NOTES

WEEK 14

MAINTAIN A CIRCLE OF SUPPORT

During the most difficult times in my life, I am grateful to have friends and some family members whom I can call. I know without a doubt that these people will listen to me, encourage me and lift me up. They do not judge or criticize anything about me. I can share the good and the bad. I can share *anything* with full certainty that my confidentiality will be held in the highest regard. There are times when these individuals need support from me as well, and I am happy to oblige. All of these people are what I deem to be my "circle of support." They are the people closest to me in my life. The people in my circle of support do not all know one another. Each possesses different traits. For instance, one friend may be great at listening, while another friend or family member might offer excellent advice when I ask for it.

You may have many friends but feel that you cannot define a circle of support in your life. Or perhaps you feel that there is no one whom you can count on during your difficult times. Seeking out new friendships can be easier for some than others. Sometimes we just want to expand our circle a bit. There are several ways to discover new friends. Here are a few suggestions:

- Attend church and/or join a church if you are not already a member. Get involved with a Sunday School class or other small group. Consider serving on a committee or offering to volunteer in some area.

- Look for new or existing groups in your area that match an interest of yours, or a new hobby you have always wanted to try.

- Support groups of people struggling with a common matter are also a good way to open up to others. Look for one at nearby churches or public facilities, such as libraries, in your area.

- Business networking groups designed to help in fostering growth and development among business peers are always an opportunity to meet new people.

- Volunteer for an organization whose mission is close to your heart. That is a great way to meet like-minded individuals.

Seeking new friendships is the first step. You also must maintain the friendship, and cultivate it. Remember that although you may have enjoyed talking to and had fun with a new friend, it is not a one-way street. Keep in contact during the good times and bad times, for each of you. Check in on her, offer to buy her coffee or lunch. And don't take it personally if she can't meet you for one reason or another. Remember that each person has his or her own schedule and time commitments to manage. Respect and honor one another's boundaries. It can be easy to become so excited about all of the opportunities with your new friends. However, be careful not to overdo it and run the risk of smothering them, and pushing them away in the process.

Having a circle of support is so important, especially when we are experiencing life's ups and downs. It's good to share your joys and your sorrows with someone else. It's a tremendous comfort having a shoulder to cry on, but it's also a wonderful experience to be able to share some great news or an accomplishment with a friend who has been cheering you on along the way. Many beautiful memories can be made during two friends' conversations over coffee.

Sometimes it can be a challenge to meet with someone or even talk over the phone. We can all become so busy, and the time just seems to pass by before we know it. Texting many times is the chosen form of communication these days. A good friend of mine and I have a standing tradition. If either one of us is in urgent need of support or prayer for one another, we exchange a simple message via text such as, "Please pray for me, I'm feeling

Week 14: Maintain a Circle of Support

jealous" or "Pray for courage, I really need it right now." It is such a great comfort to know that I can reach out at times such as these. And it is a privilege to offer that same support to her whenever she needs it.

I can't emphasize enough the value a circle of support provides. I know that there are those who do not feel comfortable sharing, do not enjoy talking to others and simply just want to be alone. Even in this instance, it is important to have someone with whom you can share your burdens and depend upon for support. Even if you don't want a group of friends, I recommend that you find at least one person you can count on; it could be a pastor or counselor with whom you confide. Everything may be going along smoothly, but it sure is nice to have someone there for extra support when you need it.

Challenge of the Week

Reach out to someone with whom you have not had contact for a while. Call her, send an email, a private message through social media or a quick text. Let her know how much you value the gift of friendship.

Strike up a conversation with a stranger in the store, at work or during your walk around the neighborhood, maybe even with another mother at your child's school or daycare. You might just discover a new friend along the way!

Focus for the Week

Exodus 17:12 Revised Standard Version (RSV)

¹² But Moses' hands grew weary; so they took a stone and put it under him, and he sat upon it, and Aaron and Hur held up his hands, one on one side, and the other on the other side; so his hands were steady until the going down of the sun.

1 Thessalonians 5:11 New International Version (NIV)

¹¹ Therefore encourage one another and build each other up, just as in fact you are doing.

Galatians 6:2 Living Bible (TLB)

² Share each other's troubles and problems, and so obey our Lord's command.

NOTES

WEEK 15

SAYING 'YES' WHEN YOU SHOULD SAY 'NO'

Kathy was tired; she had just left home to go to a meeting. It had been a busy day at the office. She had stopped at the drive-through to pick up dinner on her way home, spent a few minutes ensuring that the kids were all clear about expectations of homework to be done and chores for the evening. Kathy had managed a quick hello to her husband, Joe, as he came home and then rushed out the door to make it in time for the monthly PTO meeting. "Do you *have* to go, Mommy?" one of the kids had asked. "Of course, I do. I'm an officer and it's important for me to know all that's going on at your school." She did make it to the PTO meeting and as the agenda seemed to grow longer, all she could think about was where she would rather be. *Certainly not here, but how did I wind up in this position?*

Can you relate? I'm sure you can. I can, and I'll admit that I have been in this situation many times. It seems as though we know somewhat of the risk involved in quickly saying "Yes," but many times we agree before we

Week 15: Saying 'Yes' When You Should Say 'No'

realize the full commitment.

Reasons why we say "yes":

- Obligation
- Afraid of what other people may think about us
- Habit
- To avoid conflict
- Don't want to disappoint someone

Most of these reasons in some way point to fear of rejection. It's true, we are afraid of it. No one likes rejection. Yet this "people pleasing" behavior gives everyone else what they want, while in turn may deny ourselves of something, such as time, relaxation, etc.

Keys to success in saying "no" with confidence:

1. Be aware. Think about the times you find yourself saying "yes" when you want to say "no." Take inventory.

    - What are some of the areas that you say "yes" to where you could be saying "no"?
    - How often do you find that you are saying "yes" and then regretting it later?

2. Know why. What are the reasons for you to

agree?

- Is it because you would rather feel uncomfortable in a situation for a few hours (or once a month, etc.) instead of having a conflict with the person who asked?

- Is this something that you have been doing for a long time? Perhaps a family commitment or a long-standing tradition? Maybe what you said "yes" to long ago no longer works for you now?

3. Set boundaries. Be specific in your answer. And remember why it is important to you.

    - Don't focus on others' negative reactions to your reply, especially if they are used to you frequently saying "yes" to them.

    - You don't have to have a reason. It's fine if you do; however, answering "no" is all that needs to be said.

It can be difficult to form a habit of thinking before you say "yes." It takes practice, just like everything else. By saying "no" to one thing, you can say "yes" to something else that is important to you!

Think before you answer. Don't say "no problem" when you meant to say "no." Even answering with a "Let me get back to you" or "Give me some time to think about it" is a step in the right direction. After reviewing the pros and cons, give your answer a reason if necessary. Say "yes" when you truly mean it and are committed to whatever you agreed to do and let your "no" be one that you feel good about. In the long run, the person asking you will appreciate you being honest with them and staying true to yourself.

Challenge of the Week

Just say "no"! Be strategic about what you choose to do. Keep in mind that there will always be work and family commitments. Strategically thinking about what you do with your time instead of doing *all* of the things you feel you should will allow you to be fully engaged in the things that are important to you.

Focus for the Week

MATTHEW 5:33-37 ENGLISH STANDARD VERSION (ESV)

[33] "Again you have heard that it was said to those of old, 'You shall not swear falsely, but shall perform to the Lord what you have sworn.' [34] But I say to you, do not take an oath at all, either by heaven, for it is the throne of God, [35] or by the earth, for it is his footstool, or by Jerusalem, for it is the city of the great King. [36] And do not take an oath by your head, for you

cannot make one hair white or black. ³⁷ Let what you say be simply 'Yes' or 'No'; anything more than this comes from evil."

Philippians 1:9-10 New King James Version (NKJV)

⁹ And this I pray, that your love may abound still more and more in knowledge and all discernment, ¹⁰ that you may approve the things that are excellent, that you may be sincere and without offense till the day of Christ.

NOTES

WEEK 16

EXTEND FORGIVENESS

FORGIVENESS IS AN ACT that we are commanded to do as Christians. Although forgiveness is not listed as one of the "Ten Commandments," it is recorded in the Bible numerous times and for a good reason. God forgives us of all our sins and asks for us to forgive others for offenses against us. In *The Lord's Prayer*, we ask for our trespasses to be forgiven and that we may also forgive those who have trespassed against us. The word trespass is often defined as entering someone else's property without their permission but its definition also includes committing an offense against a person or a set of rules.

Take a moment to reflect on how you feel when someone trespasses against you. Most likely, you begin to have feelings of anger, hurt or even revenge against the other person. We all know that we are supposed to forgive someone, but it sure can be tough to do it sometimes.

If we extend forgiveness to a person who has offended us in some way, it gives us freedom from carrying that particular burden. Often, the person who created the offense against you will ask for forgiveness. The second statement is usually our preferred method for moving past pain and rebuilding trust when we have been hurt by somebody else.

Sometimes the offender will never ask for forgiveness from the person they hurt and that can be even more difficult for someone to extend mercy. "Why should I make the first move? She's the one who hurt me," we might say. "I'm not going to speak to him until he apologizes," is another commonly used statement when someone who has offended us won't ask for forgiveness.

The problem with this type of thinking is that as more time passes, the burden of the offense becomes so heavy for us, many times causing lack of sleep, anxiety or other issues, which can wreak havoc on our well-being.

The burden of unforgiveness is not something that belongs to us, so why do we carry it? Try to visualize the weight differently, like carrying a big suitcase around all day. Viewing it this way can help us see it as something that we don't need to take on; it's extra weight. We all have some baggage already and, quite frankly, we've become quite accustomed to our own bags.

Forgiving doesn't mean that you always forget the offense. Memories from the incident can stay in our heads for a long time, but we can choose to move forward. I can personally attest to this, as I forgave someone very close to me for something that was extremely hurtful to me. It was a choice I had to make if I wanted the relationship to stay intact, but the memories still pop back into my head at times. Our relationship is much stronger now because we worked through the issue. Had I not chosen to forgive, I don't know where our relationship would be today.

Many times our reasoning behind choosing not to extend forgiveness is based on a belief that by forgiving someone we are saying that what they did to us is OK. It can be helpful to remember that forgiveness is not letting someone get away with a crime against us, but acknowledging what did happen and looking for ways to move forward into reconciliation, either with them or without them.

Don't ever hold forgiveness over somebody else, threatening them or using it as leverage in any way. Even if the other person never shows remorse for what they have done, forgive them in your heart and allow freedom and peace in your life, regardless of whether or not they choose to feel regret.

It's not always going to be easy to forgive someone. People will do some crazy, hurtful things to others, but many times it is due to something inside of them and not directly related to the person they have offended.

Challenge of the Week

Perhaps you have forgiven someone in your heart but still feel the need for closure. Take some time this week to write that person a letter. You don't have to give it to them or even email it to them. Just writing our thoughts on paper can be a tremendous help in moving past the hurt that we have been carrying around.

Focus for the Week

Ephesians 4:31-32 The Message (MSG)

³¹ Make a clean break with all cutting, backbiting, profane talk. ³² Be gentle with one another, sensitive. Forgive one another as quickly and thoroughly as God in Christ forgave you.

Matthew 6:15 New Revised Standard Version (NRSV)

¹⁵ but if you do not forgive others, neither will your Father forgive your trespasses.

Matthew 18:21-22 Living Bible (TLB)

²¹ Then Peter came to him and asked, "Sir, how often should I forgive a brother who sins against me? Seven times?" ²² "No!" Jesus replied, "seventy times seven! ...."

NOTES

WEEK 17

RAINING ON THE INSIDE

It's a rainy day as I begin to write this chapter, and we all know that raining outside can be a good thing as the water provides nutrients to trees and plants. However, rain on the inside, the feeling of sadness over time, can be bad for our emotional well-being and affect our sense of worthiness.

I think it's safe to say that most of us experience sadness from time to time. How we choose to move forward with our feelings is the important decision we must make when we feel sad. Of course, there are times when our sadness is the result of an unfortunate circumstance that we have encountered, but what about those times when we are feeling blue for no apparent reason and just can't seem to crawl out from underneath the looming cloud of darkness? We can seek help from a counselor, minister or trusted friend, and there are certainly instances when seeking professional advice is the best option, but God should always be our first choice to confide in.

Because I am not a licensed medical professional, I won't attempt to provide reasons for whether or not an individual should seek professional help. What I do want to address, though, are the instances when we feel down and then allow our minds to continue feeling worse. Sometimes we dwell on one somber event and throw ourselves an elaborate "pity party," complete with hats, streamers and balloons!

Have you ever heard the expression, "Go to the throne instead of the phone"? In essence, this is saying that rather than going on and on about your problems to anyone who will listen, we should first speak to God.

God not only knows what is in our hearts, but he also knows how we feel about something. Amazingly, God has experienced the same emotions that we experience in our lives. Jesus himself encountered feelings of sadness and if he experienced it, why wouldn't we experience it as well? You may be in the midst of something so sorrowful that you think no one else can feel as badly as you do, no one can know just how much suffering you have had to endure … but God does. He knows all of the circumstances surrounding the issue and the reason you are feeling the way you do. God wants to help carry your burden.

Ask God to help carry your burdens; it is something that he delights in doing for us! During a time of sadness, spending time in prayer, listening to praise and worship songs or just sitting silently in his presence can do wonders to lift our spirits. When our spirits are lifted, we can begin to feel better about ourselves overall.

Times of sadness will come to all of us at some point in our lives, and it's perfectly fine to address the sorrow when the time comes. My husband once compared waves in the ocean to the waves of highs and lows we experience in life, and eloquently described how allowing a wave of sadness to come to us and then wash away could be healthy and cleansing. Waves from the ocean are in place to keep the seas thriving, and we can thrive too, even during times of sadness.

Challenge of the Week

An excellent way to overcome feelings of sadness is to do something for others. Offering help to others will take the focus away from your worries and help you feel better. Find a place to volunteer or concentrate on offering acts of kindness to those whom you encounter throughout the week.

Focus for the Week

> Psalm 34:18 English Standard Version (ESV)
>
> [18] The Lord is near to the brokenhearted
> and saves the crushed in spirit.
>
> Psalm 55:22 English Standard Version (ESV)
>
> [22] Cast your burden on the Lord,

and he will sustain you;
he will never permit
the righteous to be moved.

NOTES

WEEK 18

BE FLEXIBLE IN YOUR MIND

When I was 15, my parents divorced. The divorce was quite devastating for me initially. Over time I accepted it, and as an adult I can look back at that point in my life and see many good traits that I acquired as a result of the experience. One of the qualities my father taught me was to allow for flexibility in your life.

Our first Christmas season as a divorced family left me feeling anxious about the upcoming holiday celebrations. *How would it all work out?* I wondered. *How will I be able to celebrate with both of my parents on Christmas Day?* As I shared my concern with my father, he explained to me that even if we did not see each other on Christmas Day, we could still celebrate on another day with just as much festivity as on December 25. My father lovingly explained to me that there were many factors that could affect schedules, and we needed to allow for flexibility in our plans. He told me that we could celebrate any occasion at any time. The important thing to remember was that we were together. He also taught me the importance of celebrating the gift of Jesus as Our Savior all through-

Week 18: Be Flexible in Your Mind

out the Christmas season and beyond.

I learned a valuable lesson that year. My father taught me the value of time spent with loved ones no matter when it occurs. Little did I know just how much I would live into the lesson I learned that Christmas season so long ago.

When my son was 15, his father and I divorced. It seemed ironic to me that my son was experiencing the same thing that I did at his age. The wisdom from my father very soon became ingrained in my head more than ever. I knew that from that point on, I would need to embrace flexibility in my life. The time spent with my son was now going to be divided in half at best.

It was evident to me then that by allowing flexibility in our time together, my father was expressing his deep love for me. What a beautiful gift this was! I could now pass on the same gift of love to my son.

Over the years, my son and I have enjoyed some memorable celebrations. There have been a few times that I did not have the pleasure of seeing him on special days, but we celebrated the occasion at a later date, and each one was just as memorable. One summer, I was living in Florida with plans to move back shortly to my home state of Texas. My son had come from Arizona to live with me temporarily while he was in transition as well. The few months that we lived together are some of my most cherished memories. We enjoyed long conversations with each other. We talked about everything, all the good and the bad that we had experienced in our lives. One late summer day, we decided to plan a Thanksgiving meal on the following Sunday. Neither of us was sure if we would be in the same city on Thanksgiving Day, or if we would be able to see each other, so we planned to celebrate early. The holiday we celebrate in the U.S. as Thanksgiving is a favorite for my son and me because we both appreciate the meaning behind the celebration. We are both grateful and recognize that Thanksgiving Day is reserved as a time to sit at the table and share a meal with family and loved ones. I enjoy cooking the meal, trying new recipes and sharing the food. And even more than that, I love that there are no expectations or pressure to buy gifts. Everyone can just share a meal and cherish one another's company.

I am thankful that I had the opportunity to learn the importance of flexibility early on. My father's willingness to change and accept unforeseeable circumstances was an excellent example of a man who has lived with more peace throughout his life. Sure, certain times will challenge us to stand up and fight for things to remain the same. However, there will always be other times in which we don't have much control over the situation.

There are many benefits to embracing flexibility. Remember, though, that being flexible does not mean that you say "yes" to everything, nor does it mean that you should compromise any values or beliefs about yourself. Embracing flexibility is a mindset of recognizing the situations in your life that you cannot control. Being flexible in your mind includes letting go of trying to manipulate things to be in your favor. Sometimes it's best to just take a step back and practice a little more patience. When we recognize an opportunity for flexibility, we can have an easier time dealing with the unexpected changes we will face in our lives. Embracing flexibility can help us handle stressful situations with more peace of mind.

Challenge of the Week

Are you accustomed to doing certain things the same way, no matter what? Look for any areas where you may be overly rigid in your thinking. What would happen if something didn't go as you had planned it would? Try doing something a little different this week:

- Take a different route to work.
- Substitute your regular morning ritual of getting your coffee at a drive-through for a homemade cup of coffee.

Recognize that you can do things a little differently and nothing bad will happen as a result.

Focus for the Week

> PHILIPPIANS 4:12 ENGLISH STANDARD VERSION (ESV)

¹² I know how to be brought low, and I know how to abound. In any and every circumstance, I have learned the secret of facing plenty and hunger, abundance and need.

1 Samuel 15:23 New International Version (NIV)

²³"... For rebellion is like the sin of divination, and arrogance like the evil of idolatry.

Because you have rejected the word of the Lord, he has rejected you as king."

NOTES

WEEK 19

BE TRUE TO YOURSELF

A GOOD FRIEND RECENTLY SHARED WITH ME that she felt like she just didn't belong anywhere, and that she was different from all of her other friends. I can relate to feeling this way, and I'm confident that you can as well. We've all experienced those days when everyone else around us seems to be going along with the flow, while we are feeling left out or sensing that we are headed in another direction altogether. It just doesn't feel right when we encounter this type of experience, and we may begin to question some things about ourselves and our dedication or level of ability in certain areas. When we feel this way, it can also cause us to question our likeability factor with others; we may convince ourselves that the other people must not like us for one reason or another.

We all want to be a part of something. To feel included, instead of excluded, is part of our human nature. No one likes the feeling that comes from being left out of something. Much of the time, though, the exclusivity stems from a difference of opinion or belief. We may decline

Week 19: Be True to Yourself

an invitation because it's just not something that we enjoy doing. Subsequently, others may not include us in their plans because they know that we don't usually participate in the type of activity they have planned.

It's fun to be a part of a group and enjoy activities with others, but belonging to that group is not a defining factor in who we are as a person. It is important to honor your beliefs and your level of satisfaction to some extent. Everyone has different likes and dislikes, and these need to be respected, especially from within the individual. Honoring who you are and respecting what you need as a person is one way to be true to yourself.

When we stay true to ourselves, there will most likely be some instances when we feel like we are marching to our own beat, so to speak. The beautiful symphony of this world requires an array of musicians and each one of us contributes in our unique way. With all of the music of this world going on at the same time it's no wonder that everyone is not in perfect harmony.

Feeling like an outsider can be a good thing at times if we allow it to help us focus more on our values and aspirations rather than permitting the negative thoughts about ourselves to take over. There's something within you that no one else has and the world needs that part of you. Don't give in to something that is not you. Be true to yourself.

Challenge of the Week

There are some things that we just won't compromise on, no matter what anyone else says. This week stand up for something that you firmly believe.

Focus for the Week

Romans 12:2 Living Bible (TLB)

² Don't copy the behavior and customs of this world, but be a new and different person with a fresh newness in all you do and think. Then you will learn from your own experience how his ways will really satisfy you.

1 Peter 4:4 King James Version (KJV)

⁴ Wherein they think it strange that ye run not with them to the same excess of riot, speaking evil of you ....

Proverbs 1:10 English Standard Version (ESV)

¹⁰ My son, if sinners entice you,
do not consent.

NOTES

WEEK 20

TAKE AN "I'M SORRY" INVENTORY

HAVE YOU EVER FOUND YOURSELF APOLOGIZING to someone and then later realizing that your "I'm sorry" had nothing to do with anything for which you were directly responsible? Women have a stronger tendency than men to say "I'm sorry." Can you relate to any of these statements?

- I'm sorry, but I can't do that.

- I'm sorry, but I'm not feeling well.

- Excuse me; I'm sorry if I was in your way.

- I'm sorry; I didn't have time to get dressed properly.

Think about how many times you might be saying "I'm sorry" throughout the day. We apologize at work, in the store, at restaurants, to the people who take care of our kids and more. Of course, there are appropriate times that do warrant an apology from us for one reason or another. Much of the time, though, we are apologizing for things that did not have any direct correlation

Week 20: Take an "I'm Sorry" Inventory

to the outcome: for instance, saying "I'm sorry" to the waiter when your food order was not delivered correctly or apologizing for the meeting that started late due to someone else's excessive tardiness.

I know these scenarios all too well. Up until about ten years ago, I would find myself in similar situations over and over again. I did not realize how much I was apologizing until a family member kindly brought it to my attention. In my mind, I thought that saying sorry was a kind gesture, or being polite. In retrospect, it seemed that my saying "I'm sorry" might make the other person feel better. Some would even question me and ask, "Why are you apologizing?" I was always quick to defend myself by explaining how my apology to them stemmed from a place of caring, and by all intentions it did. Sometimes the apology came simply as a result of not knowing what else to say, such as when someone we know loses a loved one. We usually say, "I'm sorry for your loss," etc. Honestly, I think sometimes my apologizing made them feel a little confused or even, at times, offended. And for me, thinking that they were hurt felt much worse than apologizing for something that I did not do.

When we apologize for things that are beyond our control, it can make us feel obligated to explain in some way. Recently, I attended an early morning networking event where everyone came dressed in a variety of ways. One woman arrived a little late and as she entered the room, she quickly began apologizing for the way she was dressed. She had on gym clothes and little makeup, but she looked great! This woman is a personal trainer and that is how she happens to dress for her profession. There's certainly nothing wrong with that, yet she felt the need to apologize for the way she looked. I think most of us in the room that day wished that we could look that good and be able to work in comfortable clothes every day too!

I want to emphasize that there are many situations in which offering a heartfelt apology is appropriate. God asks us to search our hearts and ask for forgiveness when we are wrong. Say "I'm sorry" and mean it. Be mindful of how and when you apologize, though, being careful not to overuse the phrase. When we repeatedly say "I'm sorry," it can lower our self-esteem over time. It can also bring others down, sometimes affecting how they view the situation. Their circumstances may not have felt as dire to them but now, after hearing our remorse, somehow it does. We can shift this negative focus by rephrasing our words. Try using a statement such as "Thanks for your time" instead of "Sorry for taking up so much of your day."

Challenge of the Week

Take an inventory. This week, make notes of all the times that you apologize. What was the situation and why did you feel the need to apologize? Try replacing your "I'm sorry" instances with something more positive. Here are a couple examples:

- Instead of saying, "Sorry I'm late again," say, "Thank you for your patience."

- Rather than saying, "Sorry for talking too much," say, "Thanks for listening."

Focus for the Week

PSALM 18:24-26 REVISED STANDARD VERSION (RSV)

²⁴ Therefore the LORD has recompensed me according to my righteousness, according to the cleanness of my hands in his sight.

²⁵ With the loyal thou dost show thyself loyal; with the blameless man thou dost show thyself blameless;
²⁶ with the pure thou dost show thyself pure; and with the crooked thou dost show thyself perverse.

JOB 31:6 KING JAMES VERSION (KJV)

⁶ Let me be weighed in an even balance that God may know mine integrity.

NOTES

WEEK 21

TREAT YOURSELF!

As women we often spend so much of our time caring for the needs of others that we rarely take time out for ourselves. We quickly discount the idea of doing something just for us and think of it as an indulgence. *I just don't have time* or *Someday I'll do that,* we might say to ourselves. The truth is that you *do* have time and it is essential that you take the time to do some things that are unique or important to you. Nurturing your spirit is essential.

Several years ago while dating my husband, I had a standing appointment at a local salon about every five weeks for a massage. At the time, I was in a stressful job and these appointments were essential as a way to soothe my stress and relax. One evening as we were chatting over the phone, my husband-to-be asked me to go out with him on a particular night. As I quickly scanned the date in my head, I immediately knew that there was a conflict. "No," I said. "I can't go that night." I didn't even give it a second thought. He inquired about it and I told him exactly why. At the time, he wondered

Week 21: Treat Yourself!

if I was being honest and thought I must be making excuses or perhaps not interested in seeing him anymore. Later on in our relationship, the topic came up and he said that although it was an honest answer on my part, he had never experienced that and initially found it to be uncomfortable. Later, though, he realized how much he appreciated how I honored myself and my time.

For quite some time now, it's been a practice of mine to carve out time to do the things that are important to me. There have been fluctuations in schedules and changes in my finances. However, I know the importance of finding something nice to do for myself. Frequent massages and pedicures are not in my budget right now, but I can still find something less costly that I enjoy. Taking a long walk alone is one activity that I enjoy. Often it may be watching a movie that no one else in the house wants to watch. Or indulging a bit by buying a little something just for me: a cute but inexpensive accessory, and a bottle of my favorite lotion, or even a special indulgent treat. Chocolate is one of my favorites! Another frequent indulgence is to buy flowers for myself. I enjoy their beauty and the way a fresh bouquet can brighten up a room. I like receiving a bouquet of fresh flowers, but I don't need to wait for someone to buy them for me. Sure it's wonderful when it happens, but I can enjoy them just as much if I buy them for myself. Grocery stores and many large discount stores with grocery departments offer a wide array of flowers no matter the season, along with affordable prices.

When you take care of yourself, you can feel better about yourself. When we are operating out of our best self, our self-esteem is lifted. It is not due to someone else's words or actions, but only because we are taking care of ourselves and honoring our needs. Be careful, though, not to put your needs or wants above others' too much, becoming selfish. There is a healthy balance to maintain with respect to our time versus our attention to others with whom we interact on a regular basis. Each of us has certain boundaries in place and those boundaries should be respected. Remember to honor your boundaries that you set for others to respect. It is fully possible, and it's our responsibility to take care of ourselves. We need to nurture our spirits without feeling guilty. As women, we're skilled at feeling guilty, especially when someone else needs our attention, such as our husband, children, friends or colleagues. But remember that if we don't take care of ourselves, then we will have nothing left to give others.

Challenge for the Week

Treat yourself in some way this week. You choose how. Remember that it does not have to cost much or take up a lot of time. The key is to make it something that you enjoy. Think about it, make an appointment if that's what it takes ... and don't break that date. Enjoy your treat without feeling guilty!

Focus of the Week

ECCLESIASTES 5:19-20 LIVING BIBLE (TLB)

¹⁹ And, of course, it is very good if a man has received wealth from the Lord and the good health to enjoy it. To enjoy your work and to accept your lot in life—that is indeed a gift from God. ²⁰ The person who does that will not need to look back with sorrow on his past, for God gives him joy.

MARK 6:30-32 ENGLISH STANDARD VERSION (ESV)

³⁰ The apostles returned to Jesus and told him all that they had done and taught. ³¹ And he said to them, "Come away by yourselves to a desolate place and rest a while." For many were coming and going, and they had no leisure even to eat. ³² And they went away in the boat to a desolate place by themselves.

NOTES

WEEK 22

DO SOMETHING FUN!

Some of my favorite memories involve participating in an activity that I thought was fun to do; for example, I love to go ice skating. But where I live there is not much of an opportunity to skate on ice. We have a big ice skating rink in our city, but it's a bit of a drive from our area and conflicting schedules often intervene with any plans I may have of going there. So I usually don't go. In our suburb, there has been a yearly tradition of setting up a temporary ice skating rink for a few months around the Christmas season and I try to take advantage of the facility whenever I can. Last year, just before Thanksgiving, the rink opened and I wanted to go. My son was supposed to visit us for the Thanksgiving holiday but had a sudden change in plans and did not come. Of course, I was very disappointed that he was not coming to visit us. It was a Sunday and I decided that rather than being sad and wishing that I could change the situation, I would do something fun. The rink had been opened for one day and it was the perfect time for me to go ice skating. It was so much fun for me; I loved the way the new ice felt as my

Week 22: Do Something Fun!

skates glided across the ice from one end to the other.

There are many other activities I enjoy besides ice skating. Some activities are more fun to me than others. And, admittedly, some activities are just easier for me to master. Whenever I do something that is fun for me, everything else just seems to be better in some way. I feel happy, energized and confident, even if it's something silly.

Once my husband and I, along with some family members, were staying in a house near the beach. My mom came to spend some time there as well. I had bought some fun, inexpensive toys for the little kids, and, let's face it, for me as well, one of which was a kite. Previously unknown to me, my mother shared that she had never actually flown a kite, so I grabbed two of the kites, headed down to the beach with her and we began to fly our kites. We had such fun watching the kites skip up and down in the sky above the water. Mom and I felt like two kids, without any worries of the world weighing on our shoulders. I'll always remember and cherish the look that my mom had on her face that day with her beaming smile and joyful stance as she held the string of the kite in her hand.

There are many stories that I can recall which are similar to this one. Each one brings a smile to my face when I think about the event. As we grow in years, we often believe that enjoyment is reserved for a particular time, like taking a vacation or attending a special party or event. With our hectic-paced lives, it can be easy to shrug off the idea of doing something fun and instead wait until we have the time to do it. However, amusing ourselves can be simple; just taking a few minutes to read or doodle a bit while you're waiting on hold on the phone with someone can do a lot to lift your spirits.

How about you? When was the last time that you did something fun or somewhat silly? I bet when you think about it, it makes you smile. How about planning to do something fun soon? Better yet, be spontaneous with it and do a fun activity right now, as long as you are not in the midst of your workday or another commitment that needs your full attention. If you are, try it as soon as you can step away!

Challenge of the Week

Find something that makes you laugh. Watch a funny movie or YouTube clip, read an amusing story or call a friend and laugh with her as you share some things that make you both laugh. Sharing laughter with friends is healthy as long as it is not at the expense of others. Lastly, find moments in your day where you can laugh about yourself in a good way.

Focus for the Week

ECCLESIASTES 2:24 NEW INTERNATIONAL VERSION (NIV)

Week 22: Do Something Fun!

²⁴ A person can do nothing better than to eat and drink and find satisfaction in their own toil. This too, I see, is from the hand of God.

Proverbs 15:13 The Message (MSG)

¹³ A cheerful heart brings a smile to your face; a sad heart makes it hard to get through the day.

NOTES

WEEK 23

BEAUTY ENHANCEMENTS

Open just about any women's fashion magazine or scroll through social media pages and you will likely see an example of what society has deemed to be the perfect woman. A lot of the images we see have been altered, or the women in the pictures may have had some body-enhancement procedure themselves. As we see these type of images over and over, we may begin to believe that we should look this way too. Today there are more body-enhancement procedures taking place than ever before, and the requests for these procedures are keeping plastic surgeons and licensed estheticians very busy.

Before I turn some of you away, please know that this chapter is not intended to shame you if you have chosen a body-enhancement procedure for yourself. I have many friends and acquaintances who have chosen to get filler injections, a face lift or a nip-and-tuck here and there for various reasons.

The key word I want to focus on is *yourself*. Opting for plastic surgery or any body-enhancement procedure is a

Week 23: Beauty Enhancements

choice that people must make on their own.

I have met many women who have had some procedure done because of someone else's influence. One woman I met shared that she is in agony each time she tries on new clothes because her bustline is way out of proportion in comparison to the rest of her body. Her breasts are large because her former husband wanted her to look this way and convinced her that it would be a good thing for her to have them enhanced. Another woman I met told me that she initially had one noninvasive procedure done because she was unhappy with something on her skin. Afterward, it looked so good and she received so many compliments, especially from her mother who helped her believe that having additional procedures done would most likely produce an even better outcome than the first. Now, when this woman looks into the mirror, all she can see are the scars left behind from many procedures, each one done with the intent to improve on the one before.

On the flip side, there are many success stories from women, and men too, who have had good experiences with their choices of body- or facial-enhancement procedures. Not all body-enhancement procedures are performed solely for aesthetic reasons. There are many times when plastic surgery may be the only option for something that needs correction to allow the body to function as it should, or to rebuild body parts that were damaged from an accident or fire.

There are good, sound decisions that people make regarding whether or not to have some work done on their face or body. Many choose not to do anything and they are fine with it. I recently heard a celebrity state that she was choosing not to have any work done on her body or face because, in her opinion, many have not made it to her age. I think her opinion is a beautiful way to embrace the age we are no matter the number.

Whether you choose to have beauty-enhancement procedures done or not, it is important to decide to be happy with the choices you have made, regardless of what other people think. Use wisdom in your future decisions and don't spend time regretting the things you cannot change.

Challenge of the Week

Choose a day that you will not focus on your outward appearance. Make an effort to not look at yourself in the mirror during the day. Concentrate on the way you feel about yourself without seeing an image of your face or body. Stay focused on the person you are on the inside.

Focus of the Week

1 Samuel 16:7 The Message (MSG)

⁷ But God told Samuel, "Looks aren't everything.

Week 23: Beauty Enhancements

Don't be impressed with his looks and stature. I've already eliminated him. God judges persons differently than humans do. Men and women look at the face; God looks into the heart."

NOTES

WEEK 24

PUT THINGS IN PERSPECTIVE

More than likely you have experienced a time when you became upset about something, then later realized that what rattled you in the first place was not a big deal. Much of the time, in hindsight we view the issue in a much better light. Numerous things can cause us to become upset: traffic delays, slow lines at the store or someone not following through with a project or request. While these are a bit trivial compared with bigger issues that we might encounter, much of the time we become frustrated or annoyed with the situation.

Why do you suppose we allow ourselves to get upset over ordinary experiences throughout our day? Much of our frustration stems from an irrational state of mind. Rather than viewing a given situation rationally as something that we simply do not have control over, we allow ourselves to become anxious about the lack of control. When you are in the midst of a frustrating situation, take a deep breath, ask for God's wisdom and ask yourself these questions:

- Why am I upset about this situation?

Week 24: Put Things in Perspective

- Will this affect my well-being or the welfare of someone I love?

- Can I do anything to change it?

- Will it matter in one month, six months or one year from now?

Several years ago, some of my family members were throwing a party to celebrate a milestone birthday. I was at their house helping with the preparations beforehand. One of the last items to be placed out was the birthday cake. We carefully took it out of its container and successfully set it on the dining room table. We were taking care of a few last-minute details, and I turned around to discover the family dog eating off of one end of the cake. Thankfully no guests had arrived at the house yet. Our quick thinking led us to cut off the entire end of the eaten cake, with a clean knife of course! It was the only sanitary solution we could think of without throwing out the whole cake. I used some birthday decorations to fill in that side of the cake, and when the time came to serve it no one noticed the mishap that had previously taken place.

What a funny story this has been for my family and me to remember. Fortunately, in this situation, none of us became upset over the matter. This minor mishap was nothing more than an inconvenience to us. I can't honestly say that I have always reacted this way, but it certainly makes things easier to handle when we can view situations out of our control as minor inconveniences.

Challenge of the Week

Many times after experiencing an exasperating incident we continue to feed it by going on and on about the issue long after it's passed. Although it is natural to want to share your frustration with others, some situations are better if you refrain from rehashing them with a friend or coworker. Handle the situation as calmly and efficiently as possible, then let it go, unless it warrants help from others to resolve.

Focus for the Week

Romans 8:28 Living Bible (TLB)

²⁸ And we know that all that happens to us is working for our good if we love God and are fitting into his plans.

Psalm 1:1-6 New International Version (NIV)

¹ Blessed is the one
who does not walk in step with the wicked
or stand in the way that sinners take
or sit in the company of mockers,

² but whose delight is in the law of the Lord,
and who meditates on his law day and night.
³ That person is like a tree planted by streams of water,
which yields its fruit in season
and whose leaf does not wither—
whatever they do prospers.

⁴ Not so the wicked!
They are like chaff
that the wind blows away.
⁵ Therefore the wicked will not stand in the judgment,
nor sinners in the assembly of the righteous.

⁶ For the Lord watches over the way of the righteous, but the way of the wicked leads to destruction.

NOTES

WEEK 25

PRACTICE ACCEPTANCE

ACCEPTING THINGS AS THEY ARE is sometimes easier said than done. Perhaps you've heard or even said to yourself, "It is what it is."

In the *Serenity Prayer* we ask God to help us accept the things that we cannot change. But we don't always seem to know when it's time to persist in our determination to improve a situation or if it's time to accept things as they are. One way to help in identifying which direction we should go is to take an in-depth look as to why you may be experiencing this challenge. Discovering the purpose behind the challenge may help you embrace the situation for what it is. Sometimes looking at it from another perspective can help. Is this something that I need to change? Is it something that I can change? Will it help or will it possibly hurt someone else?

I have to remind myself when faced with a challenge due to certain circumstances that it does not always mean I had a direct part in it or even in the direction of the final result. Taking myself and my feelings out of the equation can help me see the situation or challenge for

Week 25: Practice Acceptance

what it truly is.

Take, for instance, the feelings that you may experience when faced with situations that you have no control over, especially those that we cannot change despite our best efforts. We can quickly become frustrated, angry, jealous and perhaps even resentful. We may have feelings of regret from past situations that we most likely have no control over now. These feelings can weigh us down and prevent us from moving forward. There are many experiences in our day-to-day life that are beyond our control. The economy, family matters, traffic delays and the weather are a few examples. Why do we have an easier time with some of these than others?

Years ago I would often feel my stress level quickly rise whenever I was running late for something, especially a flight. As a rule, it was my goal to allow for plenty of time on these occasions. So much of the time if I was running late it was due to something outside of my control. Over time I learned to accept my lack of control in these situations, and that I need to trust God and his timing in everything. This has been a tremendous help for me, and it's also served as a great reminder to trust God with all things.

Unfortunately, sometimes we are faced with a sudden, even drastic change due to a loss, illness or other tragedy. We may be so wrapped up in longing for the way things used to be, frozen in our tracks, wondering, *How can I go another day?* Even though we may be directly affected by this and see no other options, we still have a choice. We have a choice to accept the things we cannot change. In this case, it certainly seems easier said than done, especially when you are the one experiencing what may appear to be a hopeless situation. By accepting the situation and making the best of it, we may find peace and comfort. We have hope from God, knowing that He is with us and always wants the best for us.

We have all experienced situations that seem hopeless with no chance of anything good happening as a result. But through the darkest times, there is always something joyful for us to keep in focus. Sometimes our best victories and pivotal moments in life arise from what we deemed to be the worst thing ever to happen to us. It can be easier to accept a situation when we can look at it from another perspective. In doing so, we may see the opportunities and growth that came to us as a result of the experience.

We also need to practice acceptance in our daily interactions with others. We may be working alongside someone who originates from a very different background, has strong differing opinions or has beliefs that are not directly aligned with ours. We may be comfortable with our environment and perhaps complain about the differences between us so much that we don't see the gifts as a result of our differences directly in front of us. More importantly, we might miss seeing others through the eyes of God, considering them as an equal and not trying

Week 25: Practice Acceptance

to change them in any way.

Accepting things or people as they are allows unity and peace to flow out to others and within ourselves abundantly. Acceptance begins with realistic expectations about life and others, and embracing that situations in this world will not always be in our favor. Things won't always turn out the way that we hoped that they would. Everyone won't necessarily like us. None of us is perfect, nor will we ever be. And each of us experiences living differently, along a different path. That is what makes us all unique.

Challenge of the Week

Be mindful this week to practice acceptance. Make an effort to refrain from judgment of others. Whatever challenges you are faced with, choose to remain calm.

Focus for the Week

The *Serenity Prayer* is a well-known and often-repeated prayer. It was written by Reinhold Neibuhr. The prayer is frequently used in sermons and in Sunday School groups and studies. In the early '40s, the group Alcoholics Anonymous adopted a shortened version of the *Serenity Prayer* in its 12-step program.

Serenity Prayer (Full Version)

God grant me the serenity
to accept the things I can't change;
courage to change the things I can change;
and wisdom to know the difference.

Living each day at a time;
enjoying each moment at a time;
accepting hardships as a pathway to peace;
taking, as He did, this sinful world
as it is, not as I would have it;
trusting that He will make all things right
if I surrender to His Will;
so that I may be reasonably happy in this life
and supremely happy with Him
forever in the next.
Amen.

Serenity Prayer (Shortened Version)

God grant us the serenity to accept the things we can't change, the courage to change the things we can change, and the wisdom to know the difference.

NOTES

WEEK 26

DON'T LET ANYONE STEAL YOUR JOY

During the Christmas season, one local Christian radio station used the slogan "I choose joy." It was introduced by the radio station as a challenge for their listeners to look for joy during the season no matter what they may be experiencing, and to focus on the true meaning of Christmas.

Joy is not only for us to experience during Christmas but all throughout the year. We can choose to have joy in our lives despite the negative matters that may try to bring us down. Day-to-day stress, worry and anxiety about the future can all threaten to steal our joy. If we choose to have joy in our lives, it doesn't mean that we always act like we are happy. Although happiness and joy are similar feelings, there is a difference between the two: Joy is something that is more deeply rooted inside of you. Choosing joy allows you to keep your mind focused on good elements even though your external situation may not be as favorable.

Have you ever experienced a time when you felt such

Week 26: Don't Let Anyone Steal Your Joy

joy deep inside, then someone came along and after spending time with them, you suddenly felt bad? Maybe that was the time you let someone steal your joy. It can happen to any of us if we're not careful in protecting the gift of joy that has been given to us all. How about a time when someone said to you, "Why are you so happy?" Your first response to the question may have been one of defense for your current state of mind. But why? There should never be a need for us to explain why we are happy, or even joyful. However, this could be a great opportunity to share your faith and explain that joy is a gift from God and it is there for anyone if they choose to accept the gift. Unfortunately, there will always be some people we encounter who fight against joy, no matter what, and there are others who have become prisoners of fear, regret or anger.

Each one of us can choose to have joy in our lives. In fact, the Bible tells us to do so in Philippians 4:4. This verse says that we are to have joy in the Lord, always. What this means for us is that in addition to keeping our focus on God's promises, we can rely on them as well. Remembering the promises of God and knowing that His promises are intended for good is a way for us to experience joy. When we are facing a bad situation, we can choose to remain calm and focus on God, asking Him to help us and trusting in His good plan for our lives.

You don't need to wear a smile all of the time or feel that you can never express any other emotion than happiness if you choose joy. There's nothing special you need to do and there aren't any qualifications you must possess in order to have joy. Remember that choosing joy is making the decision to grab hold of something deeply rooted inside of you, and no one can take it away from you unless you allow it.

Challenge of the Week

Are you going to choose joy, no matter what comes your way? Look for joy in each circumstance that you encounter this week. Make a list of every situation and include how you found joy in each one of them.

Focus for the Week

Philippians 4:4 Living Bible (TLB)

⁴ Always be full of joy in the Lord; I say it again, rejoice!

Romans 15:13 Amplified Bible (AMP)

¹³ May the God of hope fill you with all joy and peace in believing [through the experience of your faith] that by the power of the Holy Spirit you will abound in hope *and* overflow with confidence in His promises.

Week 26: Don't Let Anyone Steal Your Joy

John 10:10 New King James Version (NKJV)

¹⁰ The thief does not come except to steal, and to kill, and to destroy. I have come that they may have life, and that they may have *it* more abundantly.

NOTES

WEEK 27

LOVE ONE ANOTHER

Jesus commands us to love one another just as He loves us. If we are to love one another just like Jesus does us, that means we need to love everyone. But can we love people but not like them? And can we love people but still be angry with them at the same time? The answer to both is yes. Love is a choice more than it is a feeling. I never fully understood this until later in my adult life. Loving someone while being mad at that person didn't seem logical to me, and I thought that by saying we didn't like someone that meant that we could not love him or her.

Reflect on all of your relationships. Maybe you have become angry with your spouse or children yet still love them deeply in your heart. The heart is where love resides. Our feelings are changing elements in our minds, coming and going like traffic on a busy freeway. They can change based on circumstances around us, while our hearts can remain in love.

While it may be easy to view the concept in regards to our relationships, that's not always the case in our day-

Week 27: Love One Another

to-day encounters with people we don't know.

We can quickly become frustrated with others based on their actions. Before we know anything about the individuals standing in front of us, we may have already decided not to like them, but what if we decided to love them instead? This is the time when we need to remember God's command to love one another perhaps more than ever. The action of the person does not always define who he or she is as an individual. We may never know the reason someone acted in a way that didn't seem right to us. And much of the time, it's not a right or wrong way based on the rules of the world, rather more of a feeling of offense based on our own beliefs.

Although it is imperative to keep our boundaries intact and not compromise our values, we must also get along with others in this world. We can do this by accepting other people as they are, respecting other beliefs and customs, and refraining from judgment.

Unfortunately, our world separates people based on many factors, such as looks, race, age, culture and class. We can easily forget that we were all created equal. It is crucial to remember this and have a balanced perception of ourselves and others. We are not better than anyone else and no one is superior to us. When we look at various levels of job descriptions, pay scales in the workforce and all the varying degrees of peoples' homes and cars, we can easily begin to categorize them into different groups. Classifying people creates separation among them, and that is not what God wants from us or for us.

So why can't we all get along with each other? It might not be possible to get along all of the time; there will always be differing opinions, beliefs and values ... but we *can* love each other. Everyone deserves to feel loved. The point to remember is that we must choose to love one another. The choice to love other people, whether we know them or not, begins in our hearts with compassion and understanding.

Due to our human flaws, we will sometimes feel judgmental of others, lose patience with someone or become angry over a situation, but we can always strive to do our best to keep love in our hearts. God loves us no matter what we say or do; let Him be your example to love others unconditionally too.

Challenge of the Week

Is there someone whom you find difficult to love? Spend time writing down the good traits you see in that person. Pray for him or her and ask God to help you accept this individual as He does.

Focus for the Week

John 15:12 English Standard Version (ESV)

¹² "This is my commandment, that you love one

another as I have loved you.

Matthew 5:43-48 Living Bible (TLB)

[43] "There is a saying, 'Love your *friends* and hate your enemies.' [44] But I say: Love your *enemies!* Pray for those who *persecute* you! [45] In that way you will be acting as true sons of your Father in heaven. For he gives his sunlight to both the evil and the good, and sends rain on the just and on the unjust too. [46] If you love only those who love you, what good is that? Even scoundrels do that much. [47] If you are friendly only to your friends, how are you different from anyone else? Even the heathen do that. [48] But you are to be perfect, even as your Father in heaven is perfect.

Mark 12:31 New International Version (NIV)

[31] "... The second is this: 'Love your neighbor as yourself.' There is no commandment greater than these."

NOTES

WEEK 28

SILENCE YOUR WORST CRITIC

Many of us are great at helping others see the best in themselves but fail when it comes to seeing the best in ourselves. We may want to try something new, but our inner critic tells us that we're not good enough so we don't proceed with the pursuit. I've been guilty of reminding myself of all my faults and past failures, and if I did not choose to silence criticisms about me, even if I believed them to be true, I would not have accomplished much of what I wanted to achieve in life.

There are times when criticism can be a good thing. Perhaps you are familiar with the term "constructive criticism." The problem with constructive criticism is how it is sometimes received; what might have been intended as helpful advice could come across as offensive to the person receiving it.

I can vividly recall an instance from my corporate work experience when our department conducted a 360-degree feedback session within each team of the department. The concept was for our team, consisting of 15 employees, to gather around a table in a meeting room

Week 28: Silence Your Worst Critic

and share our thoughts about how each of us worked together. Each person was assigned to share two excellent working qualities about a particular person and also mention one thing that the individual team member could improve on in regards to the work environment. Almost everyone on the team cringed at the idea at first, but as mature adults and due to it being a corporate-wide initiative, we all proceeded with our assignment. The day arrived for our team to meet and things seemed to progress along rather smoothly, but everyone appeared to squirm a bit when the part about improving something about themselves commenced.

Most of the participants were gracious and they did a good job with the assignment. The experience was many years ago, but I can still remember the specific things that each person shared with me about the areas in which I needed improvement. There was nothing overly negative that was said about me, each person was kind and had excellent things to say, but all that stood out to me were the things about me that were lacking, in my mind.

In hindsight, I wish I had kept the list of all the positive things, but at that point in my life, I thought it was a good practice to focus on what was wrong and work on correcting it. I held myself back from experiencing many great possibilities due to this type of thinking. Shifting my focus to positive traits instead of negative ones has helped me have more confidence in myself. It is important to remember that there will always be some things we need to work on improving, but we must not let them define our worth. Everyone has an area in which they could make progress. Throughout our lives, we may succeed in overcoming an issue or changing something, and soon after another struggle comes along. Looking at our challenges, analyzing things that we can learn from and making an effort to do our best is all a part of our continued growth.

There are many times when a trusted friend's constructive criticism *can* be helpful. They can challenge you (in a good way) and point out things that you might not see. Don't let any negative comments take root in your mind. Remember all of the qualities about you that are good. It's OK to have conviction about some things, but don't let the conviction turn into condemnation. If there is something that you would like to do better, view it from a personal growth perspective rather than as something about you that needs to be corrected.

Challenge of the Week

Make a list of your accomplishments this week.

- Something that went well:

- Something that made me feel proud:

- Something that was good for me:

WEEK 28: SILENCE YOUR WORST CRITIC

Focus for the Week

Romans 8:38-39 English Standard Version (ESV)

[38] For I am sure that neither death nor life, nor angels nor rulers, nor things present nor things to come, nor powers, [39] nor height nor depth, nor anything else in all creation, will be able to separate us from the love of God in Christ Jesus our Lord.

Philippians 4:13 New King James Version (NKJV)

[13] I can do all things through Christ who strengthens me.

NOTES

WEEK 29

NEVER STOP LEARNING

THE LEARNING PROCESS STARTS VERY EARLY for us as humans. Babies learn a tremendous amount in their first year. As children attending school we learn the basic subjects of reading, writing and math along with further development of our minds in social skills and basic communication.

Our learning process continues even after we have completed our highest level of education. Aside from the core subjects, which are required for us to receive an education, there always will be new skills that we must learn. Learning something new can be difficult; it can be challenging and sometimes it can make us feel lacking in some regard because we think we should already know about a particular subject or matter.

Learning something new can also be exciting in our age of information that is so easily accessed by the click of the mouse from our computers. If there's anything you want to know about cooking a new dish, you can find it in a matter of seconds. It can be fun for us to learn something new.

Week 29: Never Stop Learning

You may not even realize it but you are learning something new each day. Often, things we learn don't seem to be useful or add any relevance to our everyday lives. There is so much noise and idle talk going on that learning something of importance can become a challenge for us. How can we filter out the irrelevant and learn something worthwhile?

Staying abreast of current events, listening to podcasts or reading books and articles are all great ways to exercise our brains and gain more knowledge.

Learning extends beyond acquiring a new skill or mastering an advanced technique. We can learn about others by talking to them and asking questions about their lifestyle and interests. Much of the time we are so consumed with other people hearing what we have to say that we don't take a moment to listen to anyone else. Besides learning about someone, we can also learn from someone. Part of learning involves a requirement for us to be teachable. Maybe you've encountered someone who claims to know it all and never wants to learn anything new. The way our world progresses, with ever-changing rules and regulations, governing laws and weather events, this type of attitude can leave people behind while the world around them moves ahead.

No one will ever be at full capacity for learning. Don't allow yourself to become complacent with what you already know. Continue learning from every opportunity you are presented with, and remember that it's never too late to learn something new.

Challenge of the Week

Spending time to read can provide many benefits such as increasing our intelligence, boosting our memory and helping us relax. Commit to reading at least one chapter of a book this week. There's no need to buy a new book unless you want to. Maybe there's one on a shelf in your home that's been sitting for a while, just waiting to be read.

Focus for the Week

Psalm 25:5 Revised Standard Version (RSV)

⁵ Lead me in thy truth, and teach me,
for thou art the God of my salvation;
or thee I wait all the day long.

Proverbs 18:15 English Standard Version (ESV)

¹⁵ An intelligent heart acquires knowledge,
and the ear of the wise seeks knowledge.

Proverbs 9:9 New International Version (NIV)

⁹ Instruct the wise and they will be wiser still;

teach the righteous and they will add to their learning.

NOTES

WEEK 30

PROCLAIM YOUR STYLE

I LOVE TO WEAR DRESSES. I like the way they feel and the ease of not having to be concerned whether or not a certain top coordinates with the pants I choose to wear. My friend Cindy hates to wear a dress. She prefers the ease of pants and not having to worry if her legs are properly crossed while sitting. If Cindy and I are out shopping together, we'll most likely end up on opposite sides of the store as we each scour the racks in pursuit of our style of clothing.

It has taken a while for me to proclaim my style. So many times in the past, I would see a cute outfit on display and, although deep down inside I knew it was probably not for me, I would try it on anyway, just to see. But to my dismay, most of the time it looked pretty bad, in fact sometimes downright awful.

Shopping for clothes can be a daunting task. We all want to look good in what we wear and there's certainly nothing wrong with that. But many times, we are trying to fit into an image of someone other than ourselves. We scan magazines and social media blogs for the latest

Week 30: Proclaim Your Style

trends and ideas on how to put an outfit together with ease. We also tend to buy more this way. Personally, I know that I have more than enough to wear in my closet, and then some. I still enjoy looking at the latest fashion trends and learning new style tricks. I have to practice good judgment with my clothing purchase decisions. *Is this something that I can wait to buy?* Most of the time, the answer is yes, it can wait. I don't need it.

Shopping in second-hand boutiques is currently a trend in our area. I have found some real bargains from these places. You may find a high-end piece of clothing or accessory and pair it with an existing one from your closet. And what about the inventory of clothes hanging in your closet already? I recently wore an outfit that consisted of an existing item in my closet and a newly purchased second-hand item. So many people complimented me on the outfit. I thanked them for the comments, but on the inside I was chuckling a little and realizing that although the outfit may be old and somewhat used, it was still my style. I trust that the reason it looked good to others is that it was a style that felt right for me to wear.

Personal style is not limited to clothes and accessories or even hairstyles that may be flattering for some but not others. Our home décor can also be an expression of personal style. Why not strive to let your home reflect your style and your family's taste? Don't worry if you can't seem to match the style of your neighbor's home that looks like the cover of a home fashion magazine. What matters is that you and your family feel comfortable in your surroundings.

We all have unique styles. What you deem as a beautiful painting may not be as pleasing to someone else. Be happy with your style choices. Don't be influenced by others; embrace your uniqueness. Own your unique style.

Challenge of the Week

Confidence is key when choosing an outfit. Take a shopping trip. You don't have to purchase anything this time. Look in the jeans section and pick a few pairs that you like and are confident will look good on you. Don't worry about the size that is labeled on the tag. Try on as many pairs as you want to and try on different sizes. The key here is to find a pair that look good and feel good. If jeans aren't your thing, choose another item, say a dress or blouse. Remember not to worry about the size on the tag. There are many designers out there and each one uses different materials and sizing templates, therefore the sizes can vary widely.

Focus for the Week

ROMANS 12:2 LIVING BIBLE (TLB)

²Don't copy the behavior and customs of this world, but be a new and different person with a fresh newness in all you do and think. Then you will learn from your own experience how His ways will really satisfy you.

1 Corinthians 12:4-6 Amplified Bible (AMP)

⁴ Now there are [distinctive] varieties of *spiritual* gifts [special abilities given by the grace and extraordinary power of the Holy Spirit operating in believers], but it is the same Spirit [who grants them and empowers believers]. ⁵ And there are [distinctive] varieties of ministries *and* service, but it is the same Lord [who is served]. ⁶ And there are [distinctive] ways of working [to accomplish things], but it is the same God who produces all things in all *believers* [inspiring, energizing, and empowering them].

NOTES

WEEK 31

TAKE OFF THE MASK

When is the last time someone asked, "How are you?" and you knew they meant it? We long to be known. We ache to be seen. We thirst for someone to simply reach out, touch our hand and care enough to say, "I see you." Although this is what we want, will we risk allowing that person to see the real us?

So many times we act one way on the outside, but we're different on the inside. Because we have weaknesses, faults and fears, which we think will make us less likeable or desirable, we would rather hide them from other people. So we wear our masks.

When we go out in our day and everybody asks us, "How are you doing?," what are most of us going to say? "Fine." Now, if you're fine, it's okay to say, "Fine," but a whole lot of us aren't fine. Countless women are crying themselves to sleep at night over some issue, some burden, something that's heavy on their heart or that they may be carrying for a family member. It may even be *you* experiencing this right now.

When asked the question of how we are, we are quick

to say, "Fine." Why do you suppose we say this? Because we are worried about what others will think about us; we are scared to be authentic. On average, about 80% of what we hear about ourselves is negative. We then focus mostly on the negative beliefs about ourselves and use false statements instead of affirming truths. Many of us have built a substantial library in our heads through the years as we've struggled, trying to live up to the unrealistic expectations of others and our own distorted beliefs.

I have worn many masks during my lifetime, and although I have discovered the freedom from not wearing one, there are times when I still seek refuge under a mask.

- The mask of courage
- The mask of success
- The mask of happiness
- The mask of peace and calm
- And my favorite go-to mask: the mask of "having it all together"

Wearing a mask, especially the one of "having it all together," may feel good for a while, but eventually it will become a burden. Leave the mask behind, and start embracing these freedoms:

1. Stay true to yourself. When living by your own

set of values and beliefs, you are honoring yourself.

2. Stop comparing yourself to others. Remember that God created you to be you, not someone else.

3. Live authentically. Let your real, authentic self shine. Accept yourself as you are, owning any flaws and imperfections, and realizing that no one is perfect. Living this way will inspire others to do the same.

Challenge of the Week

Each one of us has a story waiting to be revealed from underneath the masks we wear. This week, begin writing yours. Reflect on all of the highs and lows, challenges and accomplishments that you have experienced during your lifetime. Recognize and look for ways that you may have kept things hidden under a mask due to the fear of rejection. Start sharing your story with a friend or acquaintance. She may be waiting to share her story too!

Focus for the Week:

LUKE 12:1-5 THE MESSAGE (MSG)

¹ By this time the crowd, unwieldy and stepping

Week 31: Take Off the Mask

on each other's toes, numbered into the thousands. But Jesus' primary concern was his disciples. He said to them, "Watch yourselves carefully so you don't get contaminated with Pharisee yeast, Pharisee phoniness. ²You can't keep your true self hidden forever; before long you'll be exposed. You can't hide behind a religious mask forever; sooner or later the mask will slip and your true face will be known. ³ You can't whisper one thing in private and preach the opposite in public; the day's coming when those whispers will be repeated all over town.

⁴ "I'm speaking to you as dear friends. Don't be bluffed into silence or insincerity by the threats of religious bullies. True, they can kill you, but *then* what can they do? There's nothing they can do to your soul, your core being. ⁵ Save your fear for God, who holds your entire life—body and soul—in his hands.

Psalm 139:14 New King James Version (NKJV)

¹⁴ I will praise You, for I am fearfully *and* wonderfully made; Marvelous are Your works, And *that* my soul knows very well.

1 Samuel 16:7 Living Bible (TLB)

⁷ But the Lord said to Samuel, "Don't judge by a man's face or height, for this is not the one. I don't make decisions the way you do! Men judge by outward appearance, but I look at a man's thoughts and intentions."

NOTES

WEEK 32

DON'T BE A KNOW IT ALL

Many of us have encountered someone who claims to know it all. Such an encounter can make us feel inferior and become turned off by what we assume to be an arrogance about the person. In most instances a person who claims to have a broad range of knowledge on any given subject could learn a thing or two. Much of the time, people feel uncomfortable when they are asked about a subject that they do not know, so they adjust their answer to help themselves feel better.

As a child, I thought my dad knew everything. Each time I asked him about something, he seemed to have an answer. The truth is that he had enough confidence to answer me honestly; if he didn't know the answer, he said so and from there used it as an opportunity for us to learn about something together.

It's common for most of us to feel uneasy when we don't have much knowledge about a topic, especially if we feel like we should be well-versed on the subject. Sometimes, not knowing how to answer is our own fault,

Week 32: Don't be a Know it All

like when we were in school and ditched our homework assignment, then were faced with responding to a question in class that we were not prepared to answer.

When I worked in sales, my team was made up of various members and each of us had an area of expertise that we focused on to help a customer with their business needs. It was a regular occurrence for a few of us to pitch our services to a client together. I enjoyed working with the team and we all had a mutual respect for each other, but there were times when I felt like I was in the hot seat during a sales pitch. In some instances, one of my teammates had spoken before I did and promised a potential client all sorts of things that I was not sure we could deliver on. Many times, I would find it necessary to say, "I don't know about this" or "I don't know the answer to that." It was not an easy thing to do, but I was firmly against making promises I couldn't fulfill. Early on in my sales career, while training in a new sales position, I saw firsthand the ill effects and the potential of losing a client that arise from over-promising just to make the sale. My trainer was a smooth-talker and top salesman for the company. Watching him make promise after promise on something I knew would not happen made me cringe. After quitting my position with the company, I vowed never to let something like that take place when I was pitching a sale to a client. There are some deals during my sales career that never closed, but at least I could sleep at night.

It feels better for us to have an answer when someone asks a question, but it's much better to say that you are not sure, or that you need to find more information before providing an answer. Saying that you don't know something can cause you to feel vulnerable at times. Most people want respect from others, and answering to the best of your knowledge is an excellent beginning to gain their respect.

Challenge of the Week

Many times we are conveying the message that we are a "know it all" without uttering a word. Rolling our eyes or crossing our arms can come across as us feeling that we are right and nobody knows better than we do. I've been guilty of rolling my eyes and crossing my arms too. This week, keep an awareness of your body language when you are around others. Even if you are not verbally expressing your "know it all" attitude, make sure your body is not sending that message.

Focus for the Week

ECCLESIASTES 11:5 THE MESSAGE (MSG)

⁵ Just as you'll never understand
the mystery of life forming in a pregnant woman,
So you'll never understand

Week 32: Don't be a Know it All

the mystery at work in all that God does.

Mark 13:32 English Standard Version (ESV)

³² "But concerning that day or that hour, no one knows, not even the angels in heaven, nor the Son, but only the Father. ..."

52 Weeks of Worthiness

NOTES

WEEK 33

STEP OUT OF YOUR COMFORT ZONE

Stepping out of our comfort zone and into a place of things unknown is something most of us aren't accustomed to doing on a regular basis. We drive around in our cars with the level of cool or heat that is most comfortable for us. With the flick of a switch or the push of a button, we can transform the temperature or lighting in our homes to the desired level.

Comfort zones for us extend beyond our cars and homes. We have many levels of support in our personal space as well as in our mind and body. When we step out of our comfortable place, we are stretching ourselves, growing and learning something new. Many times, when we step out of our comfort zone, we are relying on faith in something that we cannot see or even grasp. The story of Jesus walking on water as His disciples were in the boat is a powerful example of His asking us to step out in faith. When the disciples initially saw Jesus walking on water, they believed that he was a ghost. Peter said to Jesus, "Lord if it is you, command me to come to you on the water" (Matthew 14:28). So He did and Peter began to walk on water, but as soon as the winds came again he started to doubt and commenced sinking into the water until Jesus took Peter's hand and brought him safely back to the boat.

This story is a strong example of faith, and I often wonder if I was in Peter's situation if I would have had the same amount of faith that he did. Even though Peter eventually doubted, causing him to sink, he did initially make a move and step out in faith. That took an enormous amount of effort. The initial move of stepping out can be the hardest part in the process of moving beyond our own desired level of comfort.

If we remain in our cozy little place and never venture out, we can miss many opportunities and wonderful experiences in life. Venturing out can seem scary or intimidating, but if we look at new things as opportunities we can experience the fun and excitement that come from accepting new endeavors, perhaps meeting some new friends along the way and even learning something new about ourselves.

Challenge of the Week

Many of us have become accustomed to doing things with others around and never going anywhere by ourselves. If we are alone somewhere, it can feel very uncomfortable for us. Make a date with yourself this week. Plan to eat lunch or dinner out alone, no scrolling through your social media apps or talking on the phone while you are there! Make it a point to enjoy your meal and appreciate the ambiance of the location. Another idea for a date alone is to see a movie by yourself or attend a party solo.

Focus for the Week

Matthew 14:22-33 English Standard Version (ESV)

²² Immediately he made the disciples get into the boat and go before him to the other side, while he dismissed the crowds. ²³ And after he had dismissed the crowds, he went up on the mountain by himself to pray. When evening came, he was there alone, ²⁴ but the boat by this time was a long way from the land, beaten by the waves, for the wind was against them. ²⁵ And in the fourth watch of the night he came to them, walking on the sea. ²⁶ But when the disciples saw him walking on the sea, they were terrified, and said, "It is a ghost!" and they cried out in fear. ²⁷ But immediately Jesus spoke to them, saying, "Take heart; it is I. Do not be afraid."

²⁸ And Peter answered him, "Lord, if it is you, command me to come to you on the water." ²⁹ He

Week 33: Step Out of Your Comfort Zone

said, "Come." So Peter got out of the boat and walked on the water and came to Jesus. [30] But when he saw the wind, he was afraid, and beginning to sink he cried out, "Lord, save me."[31] Jesus immediately reached out his hand and took hold of him, saying to him, "O you of little faith, why did you doubt?" [32] And when they got into the boat, the wind ceased. [33] And those in the boat worshiped him, saying, "Truly you are the Son of God."

NOTES

WEEK 34

PRACTICE DECORUM

Good taste in appearance, good manners and proper etiquette are all facets of decorum. Most of us have had some exposure to one or all of these combined at some point in our life. As a child you might have been taught simple manners and appropriate behaviors to adhere to while in public places by your parents or caregiver. Somewhere along the way, most of us learned how to dress properly. However, others may have never had the opportunity to learn any of these.

Wherever you are on the scale, it's never too late to learn about decorum or to increase your level of comfort in its application. Basic manners consist of saying "please" and "thank you," and people appreciate it when others engage in these principles. Much of my professional background revolves around considerable time interacting with others and providing clients with a satisfactory level of customer service. I learned early on the importance of using good manners and proper etiquette. Sometimes the worst experience can seem a little better just because someone else was polite about it.

Week 34: Practice Decorum

I was in the store recently to purchase reams of paper for the computer. The item that I wanted was on sale, and there were only a few packages left. One of the reams remaining on the shelf was already open. It was something I needed and one of my items would be free anyway due to a sale, so I placed it in the cart and made my way to the check out line. When the clerk at the register saw the opened package, she was upset. I assured her that I was not concerned about it too much, even if a few pieces of paper were missing, that is a minor issue. She went on to share her frustration. "This is unacceptable," she said, and quickly picked up the phone to check if there were more packages of this paper elsewhere in the store. She was informed that there were no more in the warehouse. I assured her once again that I was okay with the purchase as is. The clerk then informed me that she was going to discount my purchase even more than it already had been marked down. I said, "How kind of you. Thank you!" She then replied that it was because I was so kind and patient about the issue. I felt very grateful to her for offering the discount, but I think that the clerk was more upset over the issue than I was and I never missed those pieces of paper that may or may not have been removed from the package.

I share this story because it is an example of how others may respond to your politeness. Things don't always happen this way; a lot of times people respond with a frown or words of disgruntlement. We don't need to expect politeness back when we offer it to others, necessarily. The act of good manners should come from a place of respect for others and ourselves.

Your taste in clothing can also display respect for yourself. Each of us should strive to wear clothes that fit us properly and are kept clean to best of our capability. Some cultures and religions have strict rules in place for acceptable ways to dress. These restrictions may have been around a long time and enforced to encourage respect.

Good taste, manners and etiquette blend well together. It takes a lot of practice to exude these traits on a regular basis. An effective way to ensure that you emanate decorum is to remember the basic please and thank you, for starters. Make an effort to put your best foot forward at every opportunity and be genuine in your attempts.

There is nothing greater than being who you are. Don't fret if you feel less refined around a group of your friends. Do the best you can and don't try to act like someone else to feel accepted by others. If you feel as though you need some help in learning proper etiquette, take the initiative and expand your knowledge on the subject by reading about it or even asking someone to share their experiences with you.

WEEK 34: PRACTICE DECORUM

Challenge of the Week

Stretch your level of comfort with decorum a bit this week. Visit a museum and take the time to absorb some of the social etiquette expected from touring such a place. If visiting a museum seems like too big of a challenge for you, try reading a book on a subject matter that you normally would not attempt to understand.

Focus for the Week

> 1 Corinthians 14:40 English Standard Version (ESV)
>
> [40] But all things should be done decently and in order.

> Luke 6:31-34 The Message (MSG)
>
> [31] "Here is a simple rule of thumb for behavior: Ask yourself what you want people to do for you; then grab the initiative and do it for *them*! [32] If you only love the lovable, do you expect a pat on the back? Run-of-the-mill sinners do that. [33] If you only help those who help you, do you expect a medal? Garden-variety sinners do that. [34] If you only give for what you hope to get out of it, do you think that's charity? The stingiest of pawnbrokers does that.

NOTES

WEEK 35

PERFECTION IS NOT A GOAL

Not having to aim for perfection in everything I do used to be a tough one for me. I am particular by nature, placing high standards upon myself and regrettably upon others at times. I like things in order, a clean home, a clean environment and neatly organized surroundings, and I like to complete tasks well. Of course, these standards are not always in place, especially outside of my environment.

Once my son had grown up enough to help around the house, I had to learn to let go of perfection. The goal now wasn't perfection but completion. I still winced on the inside when a dish had a small spot of food or the bed was lopsided, but that is not what I wanted to teach my young son. It was important to get the task done in the best way that he possibly could, for his age. Now he is an adult and living away from our home with his own set of standards. Good ones, I pray.

I still struggle with perfection; it's an area where I need to practice caution, especially with the expectations I place upon myself. God's word tells us that no one

Week 35: Perfection is Not a Goal

will ever reach perfection while on earth, so why do we all still struggle with it? We strive to do our best and that can be a good thing, but when we give others the impression that we have it all together, they could feel intimidated or inadequate in some way.

Often people feel that the only way to succeed in something is to excel, or as the saying goes, "Do it right or don't do it at all." They may start thinking that there is no point in even trying, especially if they may fail in their attempt. But isn't it better to at least try?

Once, I was asked to help out with the collection of the offering at my church, which was relatively large and had more than just the traditional center aisle. There were aisles of the church that came from every angle. When I was asked to help out, it was just as church was about to begin and I really didn't give it much thought; I figured it would be a relatively easy task. I was wrong about that. The offering time had come and as I made my way to the second and third aisles, I quickly became confused. Thankfully a more experienced usher came to my rescue and helped get things back in order. You may laugh and think to yourself what a trivial matter this was, but as you can most likely attest from your own experiences, no matter how small the situation may seem in hindsight, it can feel so humiliating while in the midst of it. Afterward, I could have easily let my humility and embarrassment get the best of me, but chose I not to. Instead, I thought, *Well, I'm pretty sure that I will never get asked to do that again.* And that is what happened; I was never asked again. My point to all of this is that although we should always strive to do our best, the outcome may not always be as we hoped. Certainly, put your best effort toward everything you do, but there will be some things that you are just naturally better at than other things. Each of us has a unique set of gifts and abilities.

Challenge of the Week

As you clean around your house take a look and see if there is any area that you may forgo or not worry about so much this time around. Are you entertaining in your home this weekend? Clean, by all means, but don't stress if you can't manage to mop the kitchen floor. The floors are most likely going to become dirty anyway from people coming and going, pieces of food that fall from plates or the always-dreaded beverage spill. Entertain without worrying about how everything looks around the house. After all, your guests are coming with the intent of visiting with you, not to watch you whisk around the house trying to impress them.

Focus for the Week

GALATIANS 5:25-26 NEW KING JAMES VERSION (NKJV)

²⁵ If we live in the Spirit, let us also walk in the

Spirit. ²⁶ Let us not become conceited, provoking one another, envying one another.

1 Corinthians 12:11 Living Bible (TLB)

¹¹ It is the same and only Holy Spirit who gives all these gifts and powers, deciding which each one of us should have.

Romans 3:10 New International Version (NIV)

¹⁰ As it is written:

"There is no one righteous, not even one …."

NOTES

WEEK 36

UNITED WE STAND

"UNITED WE STAND, DIVIDED WE FALL" is a commonly used phrase advocating unity among a population with common goals in mind. Many people in America believe its origin to be from a war song from the 1700s. The statement "united we stand" is based on the theory that if we go about something alone, we will more likely fail at our attempts to achieve victory. Earlier versions of this sentiment can be found in the New Testament of the Bible in Matthew 12:25 and Luke 11:17.

Standing firm in the idea of unity as a nation is a common theme, especially during a time of war, but I am not entirely convinced that we stand together much in many other areas. Have you given much thought to what it might look like if we as women were to stand united with one another?

It seems as though women can be extremely competitive with each other at times. There are so many social media posts from women who are bashing other women about their looks, choice of clothing or ideas that they've shared. It's a common occurrence for a group of girl-

Week 36: United We Stand

friends to be hanging out and soon the conversation leads to someone else's faults or gossip about the latest celebrity bashing in the news.

I think we've all been there in some way, and whether we participated in the bashing or not, perhaps we still found ourselves wanting to stand apart from other women instead of standing alongside them. So what does standing alongside a fellow woman look like? When we begin to hold each other up through encouragement and understanding, we can in essence stand alongside them and support one another.

A friend of mine shared a story about her small Bible Study group at church. This group is a tightly knit group of women who have been meeting weekly for quite some time now. Each of the women in the group knows a great deal about one another and shares the struggles she is experiencing along with the joys in her life and anything new and exciting that may be happening. One day a new woman entered the room before the meeting started and no one from this group had any idea who she was, who invited her or why she decided to come to the meeting. The newcomer was dressed differently than most of the other women. She had on a sparkly evening top and her ears were adorned with flashy earrings, looking haggard as though she had been out all night. The whispers about her immediately commenced; some women even went as far in their minds to wonder if this woman was worthy enough to be at their meeting.

None of the bashing from the hushed conversations among the group were verbally shared out loud. As the time came for the Bible Study to begin, the woman timidly took a seat at the end of the table. When the time came for her to share her story, mouths dropped as she divulged that she had just been kicked out of the house without any of her personal belongings by her husband of many years because he wanted to be with someone else. The only person this woman knew to turn to was her longtime friend who took her in for the night. When the woman's friend heard what had happened, she gave her the sparkly top and earrings to match as a gesture of kindness and as a symbol that she should consider herself a sparkling gem. Here the woman was wearing the only thing that she had and regarded it as a cherished reminder that she was worthy, while others were making unfair assumptions about her based on the outfit she had on that day.

This particular story serves as a great reminder for me to always make an effort to look beyond appearances, never make assumptions and offer support and encouragement to other women as often as I can. Fortunately, my friend's small Bible Study welcomed a new member into their group that day. This lady now has more friends whom she can count on for support. We cannot underestimate the value of making an effort to understand someone else's situation or the power of an acknowledgment from one woman to another that says to her, "I'm with you, and united we stand."

Challenge of the Week

Seek out an acquaintance that you would not usually socialize with and ask her to join you for lunch or coffee somewhere. Spend time getting to know more about her.

Focus for the Week

> Matthew 7:1-5 The Message (MSG)
>
> ¹ "Don't pick on people, jump on their failures, criticize their faults— unless, of course, you want the same treatment. ² That critical spirit has a way of boomeranging. ³ It's easy to see a smudge on your neighbor's face and be oblivious to the ugly sneer on your own. ⁴ Do you have the nerve to say, 'Let me wash your face for you,' when your own face is distorted by contempt? ⁵ It's this whole traveling road-show mentality all over again, playing a holier-than-thou part instead of just living your part. Wipe that ugly sneer off your own face, and you might be fit to offer a washcloth to your neighbor.
>
> Luke 11:17 English Standard Version (ESV)

¹⁷ But he, knowing their thoughts, said to them, "Every kingdom divided against itself is laid waste, and a divided household falls.

MATTHEW 12:25 LIVING BIBLE (TLB)

²⁵ Jesus knew their thoughts and replied, "A divided kingdom ends in ruin. A city or home divided against itself cannot stand.

NOTES

WEEK 37

BODY OBSESSION

I was recently attending a luncheon and as the food was served, I noticed a woman sitting across from me who forfeited her meal. The look on her face revealed disappointment as she watched the waiter serve her plate to someone else. Another lady next to the woman asked her why she was not eating. The woman replied, "I'm going on a camping trip to the lake this weekend and I want to lose a few pounds before the trip." She went on to explain that she would be wearing a swimsuit and wanted to look good in it. As I heard the conversation between the two women, I felt sorry for the lady who decided not to eat. She looked beautiful to me.

Before I could begin to analyze her irrational thinking in my mind, I was reminded of all the times that I did something very similar. I can recall wanting to lose a few pounds over a short period many times during my lifetime. I tried to lose weight by forgoing a few meals or sticking to a liquid diet for a couple of days. Sometimes I did lose a few pounds, but it was most likely water weight and it came back after I ate regular meals. I am fairly

Week 37: Body Obsession

confident that no one else but me was aware of the few pounds I had lost.

Most of the time when we obsess about our weight and how our bodies look, it is due to critical thinking about ourselves. Countless women have wrong beliefs about their body image and compare themselves to other women. It's hard not to notice someone who has thinner thighs than you when your thoughts are focused on how big you think your thighs are.

I spent years obsessing over the size of my body or what the number on the scale read. I would look at a picture of myself and instantly know in my mind how much I weighed at the time the photo was taken. I always compared my body to other women and wished that I could have their shapely legs or thin silhouette. I thought that losing weight would make me happier; I didn't understand that any issues I previously had would still be there even after I lost weight. After years of never being completely satisfied with how my body looked, I finally learned that the number on the scale does not equal who we are. It is important to accept your body and take care of it.

A few years ago during a mission trip to the Dominican Republic, our team was working with a medical group to provide routine health exams to an area of the country that did not have access to health professionals. Each patient's weight was recorded as they made their way through the line. It was such fun for me to watch the people from this tiny village. Many of the women would smile and giggle at the discovery of the numbers they saw on the scale. Most of the patients we saw that day had never stepped on a scale before and had no issue with how their bodies looked. Avoiding diseases and staying healthy were of more concern to them than how much they weighed and whether or not they felt fat.

Wouldn't it be great if we could have the freedom from obsessing about our weight like the women I encountered on the mission trip? Remember that God loves you whether you wear a size 0 or size 20. The Bible says that He knows the number of hairs on your head, not the number on the scale.

Challenge of the Week

Set aside one day this week that you will not obsess about what you eat. Enjoy your meals and anyone who may join you. Savor every bite and have dessert if you decide to indulge.

Focus for the Week

LUKE 12:7 NEW INTERNATIONAL VERSION (NIV)

⁷Indeed, the very hairs of your head are all numbered. Don't be afraid; you are worth more than many sparrows.

WEEK 37: BODY OBSESSION

SONG OF SOLOMON 4:7 ENGLISH STANDARD VERSION (ESV)

⁷ You are altogether beautiful, my love;
there is no flaw in you.

NOTES

WEEK 38

FACE YOUR FEARS

Most of us can name at least one thing that makes us feel afraid. Heights, flying, spiders and public speaking are at the top of the list of fears common for most people. This list of fear-inducing things mostly includes places, actions or creatures, but we are also becoming increasingly afraid of our situation or our surroundings. Ask people today about their confidence in the economy, and it's highly likely that they will talk incessantly about all the issues that they see regarding the economy.

What makes you fearful? The Bible has several scriptures that tell us not to be afraid. I have read many articles stating that the Bible references the subject more than 300 times. If this is the case, why we do we all seem to have so much fear in our lives?

We can still experience fear but make a choice not to let the fear take over. When we are fearful, it is a feeling that we are sensing in our minds. Many times we are anxious about something that may never happen. Take for instance, when we are nervous about flying on an air-

Week 38: Face Your Fears

plane. Our minds may begin to recall all of the horrific stories that we have heard about plane crashes. Deep down inside we know that the only option for us to get to our destination in the amount of time we need to be there is to board the plane. So we spend time analyzing and eventually rationalizing those things that caused us to be fearful in the first place. In essence, we are facing our fear instead of running away from it. Have you ever heard the expression "to do it afraid"? What this means is that you may feel scared but you are not allowing the fear to stop you from doing something.

Think back on some of the things that you have feared the most during your lifetime. Was there an instance in which you feared the worst-case scenario and later experienced a far better outcome than you had expected? Feelings come and go and we can have some control over how much we allow our emotions to take up primary residence in our minds.

When I worked in a corporate environment, my direct supervisor was in another city. He and I would have regular check-ins with each other at least once a week. One day as I was out at lunch my supervisor called me unexpectedly and left a message for me to call him back. I listened to the message while I was at lunch and as soon as I heard it, I immediately began thinking the worst. I spent the rest of my lunch hour crunching my sales numbers for the week and making sure that all of my pending projects could be easily explained and accurately accounted for. After saying a prayer and taking a deep breath, I called my supervisor back. Much to my surprise, he was calling to tell me something good; there was nothing bad to report! Instead of using my lunch hour to relax, I had wasted time, using negative energy, and focused on something that was not as likely to happen as I had thought it was.

Uncertainty is often the underlying cause of excessive worry. There are some instances that will stimulate our sense of concern to some degree. If a loved one becomes ill, we will most likely become concerned about their well-being. When our concern manifests into worry, it can negatively affect our health too, by adding stress to an already taxing time.

Spending time worrying can cause an unwarranted amount of suffering in our minds. The suffering could be avoided by exchanging our adverse thoughts for affirmative thoughts. When you are facing an uncertain situation leading you to become fearful, practice staying focused on a positive outcome.

Challenge of the Week

Fear can be one of the greatest obstacles we face as we are striving to reach a goal that we have set for ourselves. Set aside some time this week to look over your list of goals, or make a new list. Are there any goals that you've had on your list for a long time? What are some of the things that are holding you back from achieving your goals?

Focus for the Week

Psalm 91:1-6 English Standard Version (ESV)

¹ He who dwells in the shelter of the Most High
will abide in the shadow of the Almighty.

² I will say to the Lord, "My refuge and my fortress,
my God, in whom I trust."

³ For he will deliver you from the snare of the
fowlerand from the deadly pestilence.

⁴ He will cover you with his pinions,
and under his wings you will find refuge;
his faithfulness is a shield and buckler.

⁵ You will not fear the terror of the night,
nor the arrow that flies by day,

⁶ nor the pestilence that stalks in darkness,
nor the destruction that wastes at noonday.

2 Timothy 1:7 King James Version (KJV)

⁷ For God hath not given us the spirit of fear; but of power, and of love, and of a sound mind.

NOTES

WEEK 39

RESPECT

What does respect mean to you? It may seem easier to define what it means about the way we treat others than what it means to us personally. If we respect someone, we have a deep admiration for them based on their qualities or achievements. We may respect a person or show respect for an object or symbol. Reverence displayed while our country's flag is waving is an example of respect for something rather than someone.

Self-respect encompasses numerous standards and values of an individual. Respecting yourself is being content with who you are and honoring your values. It also entails standing up for yourself when your values may become jeopardized.

Mutual respect among people is essential to maintain healthy relationships with one another. It is crucial for you to have respect for yourself and preserve your confidence. When you are confident with who you are and display self-respect, it can be a natural response for others to respect you as well. There will be instances when you feel that someone is not respecting you. Someone may try to convince you to do something that you do not want to. They may try to make you feel bad about a belief you hold firm. Displaying self-respect at a time like this can seem awkward or uncomfortable, but it's imperative that you stand up for yourself. You may even have to walk away or adjust your boundaries in the relationship.

Respect is a two-way street but it begins within ourselves. The regard we have for ourselves shows others that we know our worth and honor our values. Respect for others lets a person know that you value them as an individual and regard their beliefs as well. It is essential to have a sound basis of understanding who you are and what matters most to you. Regardless of the situation, you must respect and love yourself at all times. God loves you and wants you to love the beautiful woman He created, especially when someone else tries to make you believe differently.

Challenge of the Week

Part of self-respect involves taking a look at how you are living. Make a note of any areas that you would like to improve, especially regarding your relationships. Are any of your relationships risking a compromise of your values?

Focus for the Week

2 Timothy 2:15 Living Bible (TLB)

¹⁵ Work hard so God can say to you, "Well done." Be a good workman, one who does not need to be ashamed when God examines your work. Know what His Word says and means.

Psalm 30:6 King James Version (KJV)

⁶ And in my prosperity I said, I shall never be moved.

2 Corinthians 1:12 English Standard Version (ESV)

¹² For our boast is this, the testimony of our conscience, that we behaved in the world with simplicity and godly sincerity, not by earthly wisdom but by the grace of God, and supremely so toward you.

NOTES

WEEK 40

CELEBRATING ALONE BUT NOT LONELY

It is Valentine's Day as I write this chapter. Although I am married now, I have spent some Valentine's Day holidays alone. Those times bring a smile to my face. I remember my very first Valentine's Day alone. Some friends had invited me to a "Lonely Hearts Club Party." *Cute idea*, I thought, but it didn't seem like the place to be. I wanted to celebrate in my own way, so on my way home from work, I picked up a scrumptious meal, chocolate and flowers to take home. The recent divorce had left me feeling unloved and unworthy of being loved. However, I knew in my heart that I must love myself first. What better way to show myself love than doing something that I liked to do? So I enjoyed the meal, savored the dessert and watched a classic Audrey Hepburn movie. I like watching old movies or shows with their iconic fashion and decorum. Several years later, I met a lady who is now a dear friend of mine. In a recent conversation, she shared a similar story. One Valentine's Day she went all out, getting dressed up, setting the table with fine china

Week 40: Celebrating Alone but Not Lonely

and cooking a gourmet meal. All of this for one! Cooking and entertaining is her passion, so she did the thing she loved the most and celebrated herself. You too can celebrate yourself and feel good in doing so. After all, it is most important to love ourselves first. When we love ourselves, others can too.

This practice of loving and celebrating yourself can apply to other holidays and special times as well. On your birthday, why not buy yourself that special blouse or accessory you've had your eye on for a while? Plan a party and invite friends over if you want to.

Being alone during Christmastime can be the most difficult. We see advertisements depicting "the perfect family" at Christmas. It can seem as though everyone around us is celebrating with family while we are all alone. I have had a few of those too. The best advice I ever received was to remember that Christmas is a gift from God. We are never alone because we have Jesus, our Emmanuel.

If you choose to spend time with friends or family, that's fine. Just don't let the pressures from traditions and other people's expectations determine how you want to celebrate a holiday or special day. No one knows you as *you* do. Honor yourself, love yourself and celebrate YOU!

Sometimes, it's when we are alone that we find ourselves relying on God the most, listening and praying. During these times, we can appreciate the value of spending time alone with Him.

Challenge of the Week

Celebrate an occasion, special day or special remembrance by yourself in some way, whether it be big or small. Look into your closet and cabinets. Perhaps that outfit you've been saving for the "perfect night out" is calling your name to try it out now. Or what about those dishes and accessories you bought for a party or special occasion and have never used? Set the table in style this week!

Focus for the Week

MATTHEW 1:23 KING JAMES VERSION (KJV)

²³ Behold, a virgin shall be with child, and shall bring forth a son, and they shall call his name Emmanuel, which being interpreted is, God with us.

DEUTERONOMY 31:8 NEW INTERNATIONAL VERSION (NIV)

⁸ The Lord himself goes before you and will be with you; he will never leave you nor forsake you. Do not be afraid; do not be discouraged."

JOSHUA 1:9 ENGLISH STANDARD VERSION (ESV)

⁹ Have I not commanded you? Be strong and

courageous. Do not be frightened, and do not be dismayed, for the Lord your God is with you wherever you go."

NOTES

WEEK 41

HEALTH AND FITNESS

In our appearance-obsessed society, it's common for most people to desire some change regarding their physical appearance. There are ads everywhere promising to make us leaner, stronger and younger-looking in a matter of days; some even claim instant transformation of our body by wearing a tightly fitted accessory underneath our clothes.

In addition to advertisements for improving body image, we can agonize over what to eat, when to eat and how much we should eat to stay healthy. Fat-free, all natural, high protein, low carb and no added sugar are all claims we see on food labels from the items we buy at grocery stores. But are we confident that these statements are valid?

While it's a good idea to exercise and make healthy choices in your food, there is no magic formula for losing weight, gaining muscle or toning up. Each person has different genetics and varying metabolisms that work best for their bodies.

No matter your age or condition, taking care of yourself, ensuring that you are eating healthy and getting some form of exercise is crucial for your overall condition. No set plan will work for everyone. Your friend Mary might enjoy jogging as her method of physical activity, but you prefer to get your exercise through yoga.

It can be difficult to find the motivation to exercise, especially if it's something you have not done for a while. Much of our population suffers from some type of physical limitation. It is important, though, to move whatever and however you can. Limited mobility does not have to stop you from some form of physical activity. There are a variety of chair exercises and workouts with small equipment that you can do anywhere. Make an effort also to eat the healthiest you can and try to get adequate rest each night.

Taking care of yourself is essential. When our physical state is not operating at its best, our emotional state can suffer as a result. Our bodies and minds are meant to work together; if one is out of sync, the other one may be affected too.

The way a human body functions day to day is amazing when you think about it. Strive to take care of it the best you can. Don't obsess about your body, accept what you have and be grateful for everything that functions properly. If there is anything you can do to improve the condition of your health, take the first step. This may be to schedule a long overdue health exam. Even stepping outside and walking down the street is a start to a healthier lifestyle. Take responsibility for your health and what you can do to stay healthy. No one else can take care of your health as well as you can.

Challenge of the Week

Much of the time when we get off track with our fitness goals, we did not have much accountability set in place. Ask a friend or family member to keep you accountable. Whether your goal is to walk a mile each day or refrain from eating sugar, it is beneficial to have someone there to help with your goals.

Focus for the Week

> 1 Corinthians 6:19-20 English Standard Version (ESV)
>
> ¹⁹ Or do you not know that your body is a temple of the Holy Spirit within you, whom you have from God? You are not your own, ²⁰ for you were bought with a price. So glorify God in your body.
>
> 3 John 1:2 English Standard Version (ESV)
>
> ² Beloved, I pray that all may go well with you and that you may be in good health, as it goes well with your soul.

NOTES

WEEK 42

EMBRACE YOUR UNIQUENESS

ONE OF THE MANY BEAUTIFUL QUALITIES each of us possesses is our uniqueness, which sets us apart from all others. Uniqueness includes but is not limited to a compilation of our beliefs, our genetics, our looks and our personalities. Everyone is unique in their own way. Often we try to blend in with others in a group or social setting. Sometimes we prefer not to stand out, but if we want to demonstrate the confidence that comes from within ourselves we must first accept that we are not like everyone else. No two people on this earth are alike. Even identical twins who may look the same from their outward appearance will have differing opinions and individual interests.

Have you ever met someone and thought that she seemed to be just like you? I have encountered women with whom I had so much in common, but the more time we spent together we would realize that we had not shared the same experience in the exact same way. We may say something like, "Oh, I know exactly how you feel" or "I've been there too!" It is fun to compare notes

Week 42: Embrace Your Uniqueness

about something that each of you has experienced, but her experience and yours will never be the same. Each of you will have different viewpoints even if you share a similar experience. Possessing different beliefs and perceptions is part of what makes for an interesting conversation. I enjoy participating in small group Bible Studies and hearing all of the different interpretations that can arise from reading the same Bible verse. The message may be the same, but each individual can pick up something that another person may not have heard from their interpretation. I also enjoy looking at a picture with ambiguous images, or what may be referred to as an optical illusion. For instance, someone may see a face in the image at first glance while the other person sees a type of animal upon their initial look at the picture.

When I first launched my ministry, it soon became apparent that many other organizations have a similar mission of helping women discover their self-worth. If I spent too much time looking at what everyone else was doing and how they were doing it, I could have comfortably slipped into discouragement and thrown in the towel on my own pursuit to move forward with the initiatives that had been set in place. Early on along this path of launching the ministry, I was encouraged to repeat the following words: "No one is doing exactly what I am doing, exactly how I am doing it and exactly when I am doing it." These words of encouragement have pulled me through on many days when I felt far less than adequate to carry out the task that I feel called to do.

The encouraging words that were spoken to me apply to you as well. These words are applicable each day and in almost every situation. Think about this as you go about your day, reflect on it and remember that the world needs input from a wide array of angles and your intersection is a vital component of it. Don't take someone else's place in this world, take *your* place. It belongs to no one else besides you. Celebrate the fact that no one else is exactly like you, appreciate what makes you different and embrace your uniqueness!

Challenge of the Week

Spend some time to reflect on the following questions:

- What makes me stand out, apart from others? (Think about your personality, your experiences and your beliefs.)

- Could some of my unique traits and qualities be used to help others in any way?

- Do I act the same way at home as I do at work, school or social events?

Focus for the Week

Ephesians 2:10 English Standard Version (ESV)

¹⁰ For we are his workmanship, created in Christ Jesus for good works, which God prepared beforehand, that we should walk in them.

Psalm 139:14 New King James Version (NKJV)

¹⁴ I will praise You, for I am
fearfully and wonderfully made;
Marvelous are Your works,
And that my soul knows very well.

NOTES

WEEK 43

LIVE GENEROUSLY

Most of us enjoy giving to others in some way and we especially enjoy buying gifts for loved ones. Much of the time, we think of generosity as something of monetary value, like writing a check. True, there are a lot of people who unselfishly give money away, but there are numerous other ways to be generous.

While donating money is an excellent way to make a considerable impact toward something, what should we do when we are not in a position to share our money as freely as we would like? There are several areas to practice generosity that doesn't involve capital. Churches and nonprofit organizations do rely on donations from their supporters to help keep them in operation, but besides money to keep the doors open at these agencies, many rely on volunteers for help. If you seek out opportunities to give of your time, you will find many available, often consisting of simple acts of generosity toward others.

God gives to us freely and abundantly and He instructs us to give and share what we have with others as well. Have you heard the expression, "A generous giver is a cheerful giver?" This phrase originates from 2 Corinthians 9:6-7 and references giving from the heart.

Part of being generous is giving with an open heart and expecting nothing in return. Perhaps you've heard stories about people "paying it forward," such as paying for somebody else's food in the drive-through or giving a small gift or token to a stranger.

These acts of generosity are also known as "random acts of kindness" because the generosity was shared with someone unexpectedly. Maybe you've done this for others or have been the one receiving a random act of kindness. Many times when one person extends generosity, it becomes a domino effect with those who experience or even witness the act. I've heard many stories about a restaurant chain drive-through experiencing one person after another paying for the person behind them in the line, sometimes going on for several hours.

God is so generous with us and everything we have is from Him. Reflect on all that you have and model His generosity, freely giving to others as often as you can.

Challenge of the Week

Put aside a $20 bill in your wallet or purse. Look for an opportunity this week to give it away to someone, especially to a person you don't know, perhaps a worker cleaning a public facility where you are visiting.

Focus for the Week:

MATTHEW 6:19-21 AMPLIFIED BIBLE (AMP)

[19] "Do not store up for yourselves [material] treasures on earth, where moth and rust destroy, and where thieves break in and steal. [20] But store up for yourselves treasures in heaven, where neither moth nor rust destroys, and where thieves do not break in and steal; [21] for where your treasure is, there your heart [your wishes, your desires; that on which your life centers] will be also.

ACTS 20:35 ENGLISH STANDARD VERSION (ESV)

[35] In all things I have shown you that by working hard in this way we must help the weak and remember the words of the Lord Jesus, how he himself said, 'It is more blessed to give than to receive.'"

2 CORINTHIANS 9:6-7 NEW INTERNATIONAL VERSION (NIV)

[6] Remember this: Whoever sows sparingly will also reap sparingly, and whoever sows generously will also reap generously. [7] Each of you should give what you have decided in your heart to give, not reluctantly or under compulsion, for God loves a cheerful giver.

NOTES

WEEK 44

CLEAR THE CLUTTER

Our homes, cars and offices can become full of items, many that we don't use or have a need to keep for any logical reason. How about that last item of clothing you bought on sale and haven't worn yet? If we begin to take inventory of the extra possessions we have acquired over time, we could probably open a retail store of our own. Much of the time, we have garages overflowing with items, many of which we use only once a year or so for holidays or special occasions. I am guilty of having too many Christmas decorations. My husband often reminds me about it and I quickly defend myself saying, "But I love Christmas decorations, and most women have a lot of them too."

In reality, I could pare down some and it wouldn't hurt me one bit. I do try to keep everything neatly stored away, as I mentioned in Week 35 I like things in order for myself and my surroundings. When I don't have them in order, I begin to feel a sense of uneasiness, especially if I can't address the issue as soon as I would like.

I know some people who profess that they don't mind

Week 44: Clear the Clutter

having clutter around them, but it can still affect our emotional state to some degree, no matter to what extent we are comfortable. Often, we resist getting rid of something due to nostalgia or the sentimental nature of the item.

Just a glance across a messy, cluttered room can begin the process of feeling overwhelmed. Knowing that there are more things requiring time from you can add undue stress to your mind. You may start to feel like you can never get everything done. I once heard a woman say, "I'm a failure at housekeeping!" Claiming that you are a failure in any area is not healthy for your self-esteem. Albeit you may not be as good in certain areas as you are in others, there's no reason to make such a false statement about yourself.

In addition to feeling overwhelmed or dissatisfied on some level, you may also become flustered while quickly tidying up before someone comes into your home.

Whether you live clutter free or disorder is an ongoing issue for you, your home should be a sanctuary for you and your family. It is your refuge from the rest of the world. Your home needs to be a place where you feel comfortable. I realize and appreciate that there are instances that don't allow much time to keep a home clean. Some people are living under harsh conditions or may have physical limitations or medical issues. Then there are others who are excessive about the cleanliness of their home and never get to enjoy it. Whichever category you most relate to, try to maintain a healthy balance. A home, whether a house, an apartment or a one-room rental, is a blessing that should be appreciated. This theory also applies to cars. There are thousands of people who don't have a car to get around in or even a place to call home.

The point here is not to make anyone feel bad about the way they choose to live in their home. However, clearing out some of the clutter in your life can provide many benefits such as:

- Provide more focus

- Reduce stress level

- Allow more time for other activities

Eliminating excess in our life can also enable us to maintain a healthier lifestyle, which in turn, can increase our overall physical well-being.

Challenge of the Week

Focus on cleaning excess clutter in one area this week, either a closet, pantry or the trunk of your car. Categorize each item into one of the following:

- Donate

- Recycle

- Utilize

Week 44: Clear the Clutter

Focus for the Week

1 Corinthians 5:7 New King James Version (NKJV)

⁷ Therefore purge out the old leaven, that you may be a new lump, since you truly are unleavened. For indeed Christ, our Passover, was sacrificed for us.

1 Corinthians 14:40 English Standard Version (ESV)

⁴⁰ But all things should be done decently and in order.

NOTES

WEEK 45

GOD'S OPINION OF YOU IS WHAT MATTERS MOST

Have you ever considered how much other people's opinions matter to you? In many instances, we may ask for someone else's opinion before making a final decision on something we have been contemplating. A friend or close family member can be our go-to person during these times when we are on the fence about one thing or another.

Our dependency on other people's opinions can become exaggerated, though, to the point that we rely on their opinions for many more reasons besides just seeking another person's viewpoint. For instance, if we continually feel the need to seek approval from someone else, it can become a regular requirement for us to feel good about the decisions we make or opinions we share. Continually feeling anxious about what the other person may express to us, or even what they may be thinking, can lead to an overwhelming amount of worry on our part. Continual feelings of anxiousness can cause stress and a sense of uncertainty about ourselves and our in-

Week 45: God's Opinion of You is What Matters Most

dependence. It can lower our self-esteem after a period of time.

I like to refer to our dependency for others' approval as "people pleasing." People pleasing is a real struggle for many people. After all, one of the things we want most is acceptance from others. We want people to like us and accept us. Because we crave acceptance we can spend much of our time focused on wanting to please other people before we please ourselves, or more importantly, before we please God.

Falling into the people-pleasing trap has been a struggle for me throughout most of my life. I would often hear discussions about the idea that there always will be some people who just do not like us for some reason or another. I had a hard time grasping that reality. It felt like some form of rejection for me. It wasn't until I discovered that God's opinion of me, and not other people's, is what matters most that I fully understood how free we could live our lives knowing just that. Before this discovery, I often believed that by meeting other people's needs, I would somehow gain their acceptance.

I remember feeling badly once after the breakup from a man whom I was dating and wondering how he felt about the situation. Calling it quits was the right thing to do and much of my decision was due to instances where I was not honoring some of my values. I felt at peace with the decision, but I was overly concerned about how he must be feeling. *What does he think about me standing up for my beliefs?* I had to be extremely firm with him in my request for him to stay away. One day as I was praying and listening to God, I was beautifully reminded of how much more value there is in God's opinion of me versus someone else's opinion. It occurred to me that when we are gone from this life and face to face with our Heavenly Father, it is His opinion that we will want to hear. No one else's opinion will matter to us or even be remembered by us then.

We must actively pursue approval from God in every area of our lives. When we seek Him first, He is always there ready to help us. It's difficult to make that claim regarding most everyone else in your life. Take comfort in knowing that His opinion of you will never change, although others' will. You are highly regarded by Him no matter what. Dwell upon His positive view of you.

Challenge of the Week

Have you ever attended a meeting and had a thought or opinion that could be beneficial but you didn't openly share it because you feared what others might have thought of you? Many times we are not alone in our point of view. Others may be thinking the same thing and may take the opportunity to share while we choose to remain silent. This week, seek out opportunities to speak up.

Week 45: God's Opinion of You is What Matters Most

Focus for the Week

GALATIANS 1:10 NEW INTERNATIONAL VERSION (NIV)

[10] Am I now trying to win the approval of human beings, or of God? Or am I trying to please people? If I were still trying to please people, I would not be a servant of Christ.

MATTHEW 6:33 ENGLISH STANDARD VERSION (ESV)

[33] But seek first the kingdom of God and his righteousness, and all these things will be added to you.

1 THESSALONIANS 2:4 NEW INTERNATIONAL VERSION (NIV)

[4] On the contrary, we speak as those approved by God to be entrusted with the gospel. We are not trying to please people but God, who tests our heart.

NOTES

WEEK 46

MAKE THE MOST OF IT

What would you do if money was no object? Would you travel, buy a new home or extravagantly spend your money on things you have always wanted? Most people have spent time dreaming about all the extra things they would do if they had more money to do them. In reality, though, the chance of acquiring money from winning a contest is low and there are few people who gain millionaire status overnight.

Although you might not be able to take the trip of your dreams now, you can still enjoy life. God wants you to enjoy life. His word says that Jesus came so that we may have life and live it abundantly. What does it mean for us to live abundantly? We can easily interpret this as having an abundance on earth, but Jesus is referring to spiritual abundance, not material abundance. The promise of life in heaven after we depart from this earth is something for us to rejoice.

We can live abundantly here on earth too by remembering the promises of God. He gives us so much to live our lives in abundance, but much of the time we don't utilize the gifts He has so freely given. We can have peace during a storm, gain wisdom when we are confused and declare victory over anyone's attempt to steal our joy. These are gifts from God and all we need to do is activate them through faith.

Many believe that Christians should be happy all of the time and never have anything bad happen to them. God does not promise a problem-free life; in fact, much of the struggles we go through help us grow even more in our faith. It is important to keep our minds from dwelling on worldly things. Keeping things in perspective can help to have a positive outlook on a situation and avoid making a situation worse than it is.

Life is challenging and at times it can seem unbearable, but we need to make the most of the time we have here on earth with our families and loved ones. Don't allow worry in your mind about something to steal precious time away from you. Soak in each experience and don't continue to put things off or save something for a special occasion. Enjoy your life now and make the most it!

Challenge of the Week

Take time this week to soak in the beauty that is all around you. The world is full of God's beautiful creations, but much of the time we are too busy to see the elegance of something right in front of us. Get up earlier to watch the sunrise. Take a chance to appreciate nature, people and other things you may take for granted.

Focus for the Week

John 10:10 New King James Version (NKJV)

¹⁰ The thief does not come except to steal, and to kill, and to destroy. I have come that they may have life, and that they may have it more abundantly.

John 14:27 New International Version (NIV)

²⁷ Peace I leave with you; my peace I give you. I do not give to you as the world gives. Do not let your hearts be troubled and do not be afraid.

NOTES

WEEK 47

STAY FOCUSED

THERE ARE COUNTLESS DISTRACTIONS in our world today summoning us to stray from where we are at the moment. Many people have a cell phone in hand or directly within reach most of the time throughout their day. A recent study found that on average, most of the population cannot go more than five minutes without looking at their phones. It's not surprising when you think about all of the information we can obtain from our mobile device. We can read our email, stay in touch with our loved ones through texts, check the weather and even book a flight.

Take a look around you the next time you're out having lunch or dinner somewhere, shopping or just out for a walk. More than likely you will see the majority of people looking at some electronic device, a few of whom are even doing this while driving.

We just can't stop ourselves. It feels weird if we're not looking at some kind of screen during the day. Several of my acquaintances stay on the phone the entire time they are in the car with their spouse or children, missing

Week 47: Stay Focused

a great opportunity for meaningful conversation. A lot of us even look at our phones while we are watching TV.

Aside from the distractions that our phones and computers provide, we are also distracted by our thoughts. Much of the time we cannot have a phone conversation with somebody without multitasking and knocking out something from our never-ending to-do list. Heaven forbid, we should take a few moments to sit down and do nothing but converse with someone. Can you recall the numerous occasions when you have been meeting with somebody in person while your mind was elsewhere? Or in another scenario, perhaps you are trying to share something important with a friend while she is continually glancing at her phone or asking to be excused to check an important message. Experiencing this type of situation can be annoying. It can make you feel as if the person you are with has no interest in spending time with you. Reflect on this the next time you meet with someone, especially a close friend or family member, both of whom we often take for granted.

Even as I write the chapters for this book, I must discipline myself to stay focused on completing each section. The pings coming from texts and email messages can be ignored for a bit, and I must refrain from the temptation of checking social media pages. Let's not forget the phone that needs be turned off for a while too so that I may stay focused on the task at hand.

Personally, I have been guilty of doing too many

things at once on many occasions, resulting in a memory lapse of what I was currently working on or a misplaced item that I put down and could not remember where I left it. Experiencing either one of these can make us feel like we might be a little flaky. We're not absent-minded, though; our minds are just focused on too many things at once. If we take the time to be present in the moment, we may alleviate some of the nonsensical moments we experience in our day and also be fully present in our time spent with someone we love.

Challenge of the Week

Much of the time when we go to bed at night, we are already thinking about the things we need to get done tomorrow, or even about the things that we were not able to accomplish today. Narrow your focus to three top things you would like to accomplish each day this week. If you do more, that's great!

Focus for the Week

Psalm 34:5 New International Version (NIV)

⁵ Those who look to him are radiant;
their faces are never covered with shame.

Week 47: Stay Focused

Matthew 26:38 English Standard Version (ESV)

³⁸ Then he said to them, "My soul is very sorrowful, even to death; remain here, and watch with me."

Proverbs 4:25 New King James Version (NKJV)

²⁵ Let your eyes look straight ahead,
And your eyelids look right before you.

NOTES

WEEK 48

THE BIG E

"The Big E" can refer to many things; it's often a slang term such as "The Big Easy." However, the big E that I'm referring to in this chapter is envy. I'm sure that you have experienced the feeling of envy many times. Maybe your best friend just bought the house of your dreams or the car that you've always wanted, or went on the vacation that you've been saving for and haven't been able to take yet.

There are many reasons behind envy and this the example above covers only a few of them. It refers to material things, but much of the time we have jealousy over other women. We envy the woman who has a husband or boyfriend when we don't have one. We envy the woman who has a great job and is financially secure as we struggle to get by each day. We also envy women we don't even know: women on the street, on TV or in magazines. We might see someone with beautiful golden tresses or a thin ballerina-type figure and wish that we could have that for ourselves.

When we envy something about another person, we

don't have all the facts surrounding their circumstances. We don't know the whole story. That woman with the beautiful long tresses may not give her hair much thought but might obsess over her troubled marriage. Another woman who appears to have it all may just be wishing that she could have the confidence that someone else does. Most women are discovering, on a regular basis, something about themselves or their current situation that they would like to change. We often think to ourselves, *Oh, if only I had what she had, then everything would seem better.* The truth is that most of us as women can find at least one thing that we wish was different about us, either physically or materialistically.

Part of the issue with us being envious of someone else is that we don't see everything that we already have. We may become so focused on what we think is missing that the blessings in our life become an oversight. They can be right in front of us and we may not appreciate the things we do have. You've probably heard the saying that "You don't know what you have until it's gone," and it's true in many cases. Think about how many times you have heard someone speak after the loss of a loved one. I have heard many say that they wish they could see the person one more time to tell them just how much they meant to them.

In addition to allowing our blessings to become an oversight, we also allow a cycle of envy to flow freely out of one woman to another. No woman has it all, nor will any woman ever have it all, no matter how together she may look.

Let's stop recycling this big E and begin to shut off the flow valve. It can start with you. There are still going to be days that you feel a little envy coming on, but don't let it grow into a big E. Be quick to recognize it and think about all that you have and all that you can offer others. Remember also that God may not have given you something for a good reason; we never know all of His plans for us, but we can rest assured that He knows what is best. Thank Him for all that you have.

Challenge of the Week

This week I would like you to pray for someone you have envied. You may use this prayer or one of your own:

> *Father, thank you for all that you have given me and for the many talents and dreams that you have placed in my heart. I regret the times where I have failed to recognize all that I have because of you. With your help, I ask for freedom from envy. I also ask you to bless _____. She is a daughter of yours and a sister of mine. It is only you who truly knows her story, what she needs and what her deepest longings are. Help her with her struggles and let her feel freedom from envy as well so that she may walk in perfect peace.*
>
> *In Jesus' Name, Amen.*

Week 48: The Big E

Focus for the Week

Hebrews 13:5 New King James Version (NKJV)

⁵ *Let your* conduct *be* without covetousness; *be* content with such things as you have. For He Himself has said, "I will never leave you nor forsake you."

James 3:16 New International Version (NIV)

¹⁶ For where you have envy and selfish ambition, there you find disorder and every evil practice.

NOTES

WEEK 49

CELEBRATE YOUR SUCCESS

What a great feeling it is to celebrate the success we've had along the way or something that we have recently accomplished. Hopefully, you've had the opportunity to experience one or both of these celebrations at some point in your life. It's also fun to celebrate the success of someone else. Sometimes that is easier for us to do. In some instances, we have become accustomed to shrugging off a major achievement as if it's nothing special. Maybe you've heard the saying, "If we don't pat ourselves on the back, who will?"

Patting ourselves on the back may sound a little cliché. It's true, though, in some way because if we are waiting around for someone to acknowledge all of the great things we are doing, then we could be waiting a long time. Acknowledging ourselves can feel like we are bragging about ourselves. But if we can reframe how we view the concept, we can maintain a strong symmetry in how we look at celebrating ourselves and our accomplishments.

I have been asked to share my greatest achievement

Week 49: Celebrate Your Success

in life or something that I was most proud of on some occasions. Both are frequently asked during job interviews. I suspect it is to gain more insight into the person's ambitions and perhaps their values as well. Many people have a difficult time answering these questions.

Let's put everything into perspective. If you are at a social gathering and going on and on about all of the success in your life and your recent accomplishments, that can come across the wrong way. It can seem to others as though you are bragging. If, however, it is in another setting such as a job interview it is simply to learn more about you as a potential employee.

What about those times when you feel like there is a reason to celebrate but no one else around you feels that way? It's OK to feel happy and excited about things even if others around you don't share your joy, and even if others try to bring you down as sometimes is the case.

One year after launching my ministry, I had accomplished the task of creating curriculum and scheduling and facilitating my very first workshop. That was a huge achievement for me. Immediately after the seminar I began to dissect all of the elements. What went well? What could have gone better? The next day I felt tired. I decided then that I should put the analyzing away for a day and celebrate my success in some way. I did celebrate, and it wasn't in a big way, just something special to me. I also found a memorable way to mark the achievement. Later on, I had a photo of our group from the workshop framed and added a title at the bottom "First Workshop," along with the date of the seminar.

That day holds an enormous amount of significance for me. It always will. Of course, there are things that I have learned along the way to make each workshop and event better than the previous one. But the point is that I did what I set out to do. It was an accomplishment, and that was a reason to celebrate!

Challenge of the Week

How about you? Do you have something to celebrate? Think about everything you have set out to do and then completed. Think about all of the times that God has helped you in reaching a goal. Even setting a goal to drink a full 6-8 glasses of water a day is something to celebrate. I hope that you will find many reasons to celebrate!

Focus for the Week

ECCLESIASTES 3:13 LIVING BIBLE (TLB)

¹³ and second, that he should eat and drink and enjoy the fruits of his labors, for these are gifts from God.

LUKE 15:23-24 ENGLISH STANDARD VERSION (ESV)

²³ And bring the fattened calf and kill it, and let us eat and celebrate. ²⁴ For this my son was dead, and is alive again; he was lost, and is found.' And they began to celebrate.

2 Chronicles 5:12-14 New King James Version (NKJV)

¹² and the Levites who were the singers, all those of Asaph and Heman and Jeduthun, with their sons and their brethren, stood at the east end of the altar, clothed in white linen, having cymbals, stringed instruments and harps, and with them one hundred and twenty priests sounding with trumpets— ¹³ indeed it came to pass, when the trumpeters and singers were as one, to make one sound to be heard in praising and thanking the Lord, and when they lifted up their voice with the trumpets and cymbals and instruments of music, and praised the Lord, saying:

"*For He is* good,
For His mercy *endures* forever,"

that the house, the house of the Lord, was filled with a cloud, ¹⁴ so that the priests could not continue ministering because of the cloud; for the glory of the Lord filled the house of God.

NOTES

WEEK 50

IT'S NOT ALWAYS ABOUT BEING RIGHT

RELATIONSHIPS ARE IMPORTANT. Jesus showed us that by his example of always taking the time to talk with others. There are many types of relationships. Family, work, church groups and other social groups are places where we develop friends and acquaintances, the most common types of relationships. It can be difficult at times to maintain peace among all your relationships, especially with those who are closest to us. I think we have all experienced strife with someone along the way, usually stemming from a mindset of who was right in the first place. These arguments can turn into a game of "he said, she said," going round and round with no resolution. That can be so frustrating. You know you are right, there is no doubt in your mind; in fact, you even have proof! But the other person is so convinced that he or she is right as well, and with the same amount of conviction.

Arguing with someone to the point of exhaustion over an issue can cause so much stress and hurt. The more we hear the other person stating their case against

Week 50: It's Not Always About Being Right

us, the more we become defensive, frustrated and angry. In these experiences, we need to step outside for a moment and look at what the relationship means to us, instead of what the argument is about. *Is this something that will matter later on? Do I want to risk my relationship with this person for the sake of winning an argument?* It's certainly not an easy thing to do. But think about these things. I'm not advising you just to surrender and throw in the towel, so to speak. However, you can change the course of events to move into a more loving and peaceful discussion. You may even agree to disagree but still love and respect each other. It's not about being right. It's about keeping a relationship that matters to you fully intact.

My sister and I are extremely close and we have had some pretty hefty arguments over the years, but we both value our relationship more than anything else. Each of us agrees that our relationship is more important than one of us winning an argument. And most of the issues we have argued about were trivial and now long forgotten.

Our time here on earth is short-lived. We never know how long it will be, and we never know how long we have to spend with family and friends. Many are living with regret about a strained relationship that they never had the opportunity to mend. Don't let that happen to you.

Our relationships are vital to our emotional well-being. We were created to be in community with others. If you do not feel as if you have any personal relationships,

I pray that you know you are not alone. You can always have a personal relationship with Christ, the ultimate companion.

Challenge of the Week

Be mindful of your conversations and behavior with others. Could the discussion you are engaged in, which is bordering on argument status, merely be a disagreement between two peers with different opinions, or perhaps two people who see the situation from different perspectives?

Focus for the Week

> Ephesians 4:2-3 New International Version (NIV)
>
> ² Be completely humble and gentle; be patient, bearing with one another in love. ³ Make every effort to keep the unity of the Spirit through the bond of peace.
>
> Proverbs 18:24 New King James Version (NKJV)
>
> ²⁴ A man *who has* friends must himself be friendly, But there is a friend *who* sticks closer than a brother.

Week 50: It's Not Always About Being Right

Leviticus 19:18 New International Version (NIV)

¹⁸ "'Do not seek revenge or bear a grudge against anyone among your people, but love your neighbor as yourself. I am the Lord.

NOTES

WEEK 51

KNOW YOUR LIMITATIONS

"I'M SO TIRED," JANICE SAID TO HER FRIEND as the two of them were entering the daycare to pick up each of their kids after work. Janice went on to explain how she felt overwhelmed and did not know how she could get everything done that she needed to this week. Between her work, family and other commitments, Janice felt stretched beyond her limits.

We have all had days and even entire weeks or longer that left us feeling like we had stretched ourselves beyond our limits. It can become an everyday occurrence, and before we even realize it we can become exhausted. Often, we are way in over our heads and feeling overwhelmed before we finally admit that we may be doing too much.

Admitting that we are in over our heads is not always so easy to do, but it is crucial for us to recognize our limitations. Recognizing that we are headed to a place that is beyond our abilities is the first step in helping us to avoid the feeling of being overwhelmed.

Many times it's too late for us to decline a request or

Week 51: Know Your Limitations

ask for help with the task or responsibility we have agreed to complete. When this is the case, it can be helpful to take a look at your commitments and to-do lists and begin to categorize them. Is there anything that I have to do that I could ask for someone's help? Can something be pushed back to a later date for completion?

Besides these questions, ask yourself why you are doing something. Did you sign up for that cake decorating class because your friend is always making beautiful cakes for her daughter's birthday celebrations and you would like to do the same thing for your son's parties?

Many times we tackle something because we like the challenge and that is OK. Just make certain that you are creating this challenge for yourself to learn something new or grow in an area that you would like to expand on. Don't take on another project with the intent of becoming more like someone else. Each person has different talents and abilities, as well as varying limitations on their bodies, minds and time.

A wonderful friend of mine from high school was very athletic, while I did not possess any athletic abilities at all. I would always admire her talent and strong physique so one year I decided to try out for softball, which I didn't particularly enjoy. I was afraid of being hit by the ball, even though it was not a hardball that we used in the game. The day for team tryouts arrived and it was one of the warmest days on record for that time of year. I was already miserable as I was beginning to sweat and itch from the helmet while waiting to bat. Deep inside I knew that this was not for me, but I forged on anyway. Now at the home plate and ready to attempt to hit the ball ... strike 1, 2 and 3, and then a loud distant yelling of "You're out" took place before I realized it. Next came time for me to be in the outfield and during the first inning the ball came directly at me and hit me in the thigh. "Ouch!" I said to myself and vowed then and there that I would never again attempt to play on the softball team.

This story is one lesson of many that I have learned through the years, and with each one I learn more about my limitations and how important it is first, to recognize them, and second, to admit them and stay within my limits. By respecting my limitations, I am honoring my talents and strengths, and will feel more satisfied about the things I can accomplish.

Challenge of the Week

Look at all of your current commitments. Is there anything that you can delegate to someone else or ask for help? If not now, perhaps three months or even six months from now? Envision how you would like your schedule to look six months from now, list anything that you could scale down or omit altogether and then make it a goal to adjust your schedule accordingly.

Week 51: Know Your Limitations

Focus for the Week

MATTHEW 11:28-30 ENGLISH STANDARD VERSION (ESV)

²⁸ Come to me, all who labor and are heavy laden, and I will give you rest. ²⁹ Take my yoke upon you, and learn from me, for I am gentle and lowly in heart, and you will find rest for your souls. ³⁰ For my yoke is easy, and my burden is light."

COLOSSIANS 3:23 REVISED STANDARD VERSION (RSV)

²³ Whatever your task, work heartily, as serving the Lord and not men ....

NOTES

WEEK 52

LEAVE A LEGACY

Often when we hear the word "legacy," we think of someone much older, who has lived a long time and experienced many things in life. But no matter your age, you can begin to leave a legacy for someone else. I hadn't given this much thought until recently when I had some time to myself, sitting around a public pool on a weekend getaway. The trip was over a holiday weekend so many people were swimming at the pool on this particular day. As I looked around watching all of the different families and groups of people, I overheard a lot of conversations. None of them seemed to be discussing anything confidential, just simple chats among friends and loved ones. From observing and listening to others, especially women, I realized that each generation has a little something different to offer to others. Older women can share stories from their past, which can leave a lasting impression on a younger friend or family member. Young ladies and mothers can set the standard for girls who are at an impressionable age and are seeking examples of how to conduct themselves once they become

Week 52: Leave a Legacy

young women.

Being role models for other women is something that we can all do each day of our lives. There is no need to wait until we are older or wiser, or even until we feel that we have more to offer to someone else. We don't even have to know anyone who may be in search of a mentor. Countless women need someone to leave a legacy for them, someone they can look up to and respect. Many young girls are looking at scantily clothed women on magazine covers as their role models. There are a lot of girls, and women, who have never had the opportunity to learn how to dress fashionably without being too far out in their choices, and many others who have missed altogether learning to have respect for themselves.

Understanding how to leave a legacy for someone we know and love can be easy, but how can we leave a legacy for someone we don't know personally? One way to begin this task is to stop judging a person by what we see on the outside. We can be quick to judge other women based on how they dress or act in public, but we don't know what's on the inside or what they may have experienced in their lives.

The definition of a legacy is a gift, an heirloom, an endowment or a tradition. By leaving a legacy for someone, we are giving a gift and also leaving them with a lasting impression. When we make an impact on someone, we want the impression to be a good one instead of a bad one. The words we say to a woman can bring her up or tear her down, and our example to others can have the same effect regarding a person's feelings about herself.

Think about leaving a legacy as leaving your mark on this world. What did you do while you were living your life on earth? Were you able to help someone, give sound advice to someone who was in need of it or make a difference in the life of someone else? The act of leaving a legacy doesn't have to be a huge thing, just a simple acknowledgment of someone who often is overlooked is a big deal. Extending kindness or a genuine smile to others is another effortless way to leave a lasting impression, and one that can easily be passed along to others.

Challenge of the Week

Next time you are out, look for an opportunity to compliment another woman. Don't go out of your way and make yourself do it if it's not in you to do so; you must be genuine in your approach. It could be as you are waiting in line for coffee and you see a lady with an outfit that you just love. Compliment her and tell her how much you like it or how great the outfit looks on her.

Focus for the Week

PSALM 78:1-4 THE MESSAGE (MSG)

¹ Listen, dear friends, to God's truth,

Week 52: Leave a Legacy

bend your ears to what I tell you.

² I'm chewing on the morsel of a proverb;

I'll let you in on the sweet old truths,

³ Stories we heard from our fathers,

counsel we learned at our mother's knee.

⁴ We're not keeping this to ourselves,

we're passing it along to the next generation—

GOD's fame and fortune,

the marvelous things he has done.

Proverbs 13:22 Revised Standard Version (RSV)

²² A good man leaves an inheritance to his children's children,

but the sinner's wealth is laid up for the righteous.

NOTES

ACKNOWLEDGMENTS

Writing a book is one task, completing it is another. The desire to write this book came from within but making the dream a reality required much outside help and support from others.

First and foremost, all praise to our Heavenly Father who placed the desire in my heart to write a book. I am grateful for His unending love and patience during my many years of procrastination in answering the call. Without His grace and wisdom, the completion of this book would not have been possible.

Words cannot express the heartfelt appreciation I have for my husband and family. Thanks to each one of you for loving me unconditionally, believing in me and supporting me. Special thanks for extending grace when I chose to exchange time spent with you for time spent in front of the computer. I am grateful for the gift of my family; I love you all.

I am forever grateful to my dear friend Susan Hulburt,

who unselfishly gave of her time to serve as copy editor. Sincere thanks to Julie Osterman, who also worked as copy editor, adding finesse to my words and encouragement along the way. What a blessing it was to work with such well-informed women, both of whom understood the message I wanted to convey and allowed my voice to come through with more clarity. Their guidance and expertise throughout the process expanded my writing skills and knowledge significantly.

Deepest gratitude to Kim Hester at Passionvine Creative, who worked as graphic designer for the book cover and interior layout. It was such a pleasure to work with Kim on this project. Her remarkable eye for design and focus on details never missed the mark in producing a superior product. Working with Kim was also a blessing; she too understood the message of my book and amazingly, had the gift to see my vision as if she were viewing it through my eyes.

And last but certainly not least, a tremendous thank you to all of my friends for sharing my enthusiasm and providing encouragement, especially during my times of weariness or doubt. You are all a gift to me, and I love each one of you.

www.ingramcontent.com/pod-product-compliance
Lightning Source LLC
Chambersburg PA
CBHW050528300426
44113CB00012B/1997